Veterans Benefits
for the
Florida Resident

JOHN R. FRAZIER, J.D., LL.M.
JOSEPH F. PIPPEN, JR., J.D.

Cabo Azul
Publications, LLC

F L O R I D A

Veterans Benefits for the Florida Resident
© 2017 by John R. Frazier J.D., LL.M.

Softcover ISBN 978-0-9907940-2-8
EPUB eBook ISBN 978-0-9907940-3-5

Published by
Cabo Azul Publications, LLC
10225 Ulmerton Road, Bldg. #11
Largo, FL 33771
Phone: (727) 586-3306, ext. 104
Fax: (727) 586-6276

Author's Website
EstateLegalPlanning.com

Individuals' Orders
Amazon.com
AllBookStores.com
(search by ISBN, then choose "compare prices")

First Edition 2017

Written, produced and printed in the United States of America.

To the brave men and women
who have served in the
United Sates Armed Forces
to protect the American way of life

To my parents, J. Richard Frazier and Anne R. Frazier,
and my grandparents, Richard O. Frazier and Marian R. Frazier,
whose life-long dedication to higher education
served as an inspiration for this book.

Contents

Acknowledgments

A special appreciation is due my mentor and friend Joseph F. Pippen, Jr. for his wisdom and guidance throughout my legal career.

I also wish to thank my friend Henry Harlow, for helping me set my goals high and keep balance in life.

Lastly, heartfelt thanks to my publisher Betsy Lampe and her key team members at Rainbow Books, who have brought my vision to life.

Introduction to
Veterans Benefits

If you are a veteran living in the State of Florida, you are in the company of over 1.6 million other men and women who have honorably served our country. And, as a veteran of the United States Armed Forces, or as the surviving spouse of a veteran, you may be eligible for various benefits and services provided by the U.S. Department of Veterans Affairs (VA).

Most veterans are aware of the basic education, health care and housing benefits the VA offers. Still, many veterans and their families do not know about some lesser-known yet extremely important programs— benefits providing financial help that can better the lives of disabled or elderly veterans and their loved ones, while greatly reducing otherwise crippling costs.

As a veterans advocate, I present this book to help ensure Florida veterans get a fair deal. In the following chapters we will focus on two general categories of Veterans Benefits:

- Service Connected Benefits (Disability Compensation) — a monetary benefit paid to veterans who are disabled due to injuries or disease sustained or aggravated during active military service. Eligibility is based on service requirements and service connected disability requirements, and not on income.

- Non-Service Connected Benefits (Pension) — a monetary benefit paid to senior or disabled veterans with financial needs and who served on active duty at least 90 days, with one of those days during a period of war. Combat service is not a requirement. Pension is also available to eligible survivors. Eligibility is based on service requirements, income and net worth restrictions, and disability and/or age requirements.

Many veterans are already familiar with disability compensation (service connected) benefits. Chapter 2 helps explain this important compensation program, how to get started and what to expect.

On the other hand, countless wartime veterans are totally unaware that, if they are 65 or older and on a limited income, they may be eligible for VA Pension benefits without being disabled or even if their disability or illness is unrelated to military service. Chapter 3 reveals this valuable non-service connected pension benefit and what it may mean for you, your family and for certain survivors of deceased veterans.

With both Service Connected Disability Compensation and Non-Service Connected Pension, benefits are contingent on the veteran's discharge being other than dishonorable. A disabled veteran can choose only one benefit; therefore, he or she must evaluate each program to know which benefit is more appropriate in his or her individual case.

The Importance of Veterans Benefits
for Florida Residents

In 1975, there were two million veterans over the age of 65. By 2017, that number is expected to be near 10 million. Representing senior or disabled veterans in connection with veterans benefit claims is an area of increasing importance in the practice of law, and specifically veterans pension and Medicaid planning.

The costs of long-term care can be impoverishing. For elderly veterans who need to plan for their long-term care, or whose health care expenses exceed their income, VA Pension and related Medicaid benefits can significantly assist those who qualify. If the veteran (or the surviving spouse of a deceased veteran) is also applying for Medicaid in Florida, the Department of Children and Families (DCF) will require the veteran to submit an application for Veterans Benefits with the VA before any Medicaid benefits are awarded. Medicaid is considered the provider of last resort.

These are complex areas of law that often call for qualified legal counsel to ethically and insightfully advise Florida veterans about their choices.

Records show that, as of 2016, Florida holds the third largest population of veterans in the U.S. Because many of these veterans served in World War II, Korea and Vietnam, Florida leads the way for residents 65 and older. Consider these statistics:

- 1.2 million wartime veterans make up about 75 percent of Florida's total veteran population.
- There are more Vietnam-era veterans than any other wartime category in Florida, with more than 498,000 veterans.
- More than 231,000 Afghanistan and Iraq War veterans claim Florida as their home.
- Florida has more than 160,000 women veterans.

- Florida has the largest population of World War II veterans in the nation (over 164,000).
- Florida has the third largest population of disabled veterans in the nation (more than 249,000).
- Florida has more than 731,000 veterans over the age of 65.
- 187,000 military retirees call Florida home.[1]

Our wounded, aging and disabled veterans need efficient access to the benefits they deserve. Financial aid exists for veterans with and without service connected disabilities.

For generations, our country's men and women have served the United States with courage and commitment as members of America's Armed Forces. As an attorney, I am accredited by the Department of Veterans Affairs to prepare, present and prosecute claims for veterans before the VA. It is with great respect and honor for their service and sacrifice to our country that I represent our local veterans.

This book is a resource for Florida veterans, their families and loved ones. If you reach for this book, chances are you need answers to specific questions. While the chapters within cannot replace a lawyer's personal advice, they do provide a solid introduction to these important programs. Please use this information as a starting point to access the benefits you need.

Chapter 1

The History and Background of the U.S. Department of Veterans Affairs

From the War of Independence to the campaign in Afghanistan, the history of the United States Department of Veterans Affairs (VA) is an enlightening account of how a single entity evolved solely to assist our nation's veterans. A basic understanding of the VA's story is important in understanding its role, not only as a government program, but in the lives of millions of veterans and their families — past, present and future.

What Is the Department of Veterans Affairs?

The U.S. Department of Veterans Affairs is a federal military veterans benefit program. The VA is part of the U.S. Cabinet, which includes the Vice President and the heads of 15 executive departments.

Many assume that Veterans Affairs is part of the Department of Defense (DOD), which oversees our nation's military system. However,

The VA and DOD are separate, independent systems — even when it comes to health care.

Veteran's law is located in Title 38 of the United States Code (USC), "Veterans' Benefits." Related regulations regarding VA benefits issued by the Secretary of Veterans Affairs are contained in Title 38, Code of Federal Regulations (CFR), "Pensions, Bonuses and Veterans Relief."

The VA is comprised of three main administrative divisions:

1. *Veterans Health Administration* (VHA) — provides medical care to veterans through integrated health care services, including VA Medical Centers, clinics and nursing home aid.

2. *Veterans Benefits Administration* (VBA) — provides financial assistance, such as VA Pension (Aid and Attendance) and VA Disability Compensation, and other benefits to veterans, their dependents and survivors.

3. *National Cemetery Administration* (NCA) — evolving since the Civil War, the NCA honors veterans and their families with final resting places. NCA maintains 135 national cemeteries in 40 states and other sites.

If you are filing a claim for Veterans Benefits, you will deal with the Veterans Benefits Administration. The VBA is divided into Regional Districts: North Atlantic, Southeast, Midwest, Continental and Pacific. The Regional Benefit Office for Florida residents is located in St. Petersburg, Florida.

Each state (or territory) also has its own State Veterans Affairs Office. For Florida residents, the Florida Department of Veterans Affairs is located in Largo and may be contacted through FloridaVets.org or by calling (727) 518-3202.

Why Was the VA Created?

The United States has cared for veteran's needs, in some manner, for more than 380 years. The massive system that is now "Veterans Affairs" evolved in response to each new period of war, providing critical respite and aid to veterans wounded in battle or stricken by disease. It was the serviceable response to veterans returning from wars in numbers that threatened to overwhelm the civilian health care system.

The story of how Veterans Benefits would develop, who would qualify for them and how these provisions would be governed evolved along with our country. Today, the VA's mission statement reflects Abraham Lincoln's initial vision during the Civil War:

> "To care for him who shall have borne the battle, and for his widow, and his orphan" by serving and honoring the men and women who are America's Veterans."[2]

The veteran population has soared since the first battle in colonial times. Veterans benefits have magnified in both scope and size, reaching beyond pensions and disability compensation and into burial, health care, research, education and vocational training.

How Is the VA Funded?

In a nutshell, our federal income tax dollars help pay federally funded programs, including those administered by the Department of Veterans Affairs.

The VA sends its annual budget request to Congress for the resources needed to maintain its three main branches, increase veteran access to benefits and services, sustain progress on removing the disability claims backlog, and for ending veteran homelessness.

The President's 2017 Budget includes $182.3 billion for the VA in 2017. This includes $78.7 billion in discretionary resources and $103.6 billion in mandatory funding.[3]

Then there is the "elephant in the room" — known as the budget deficit. The money the federal government borrows to cover the budget deficit is what creates the national debt, which stands just under $20 trillion at the time of this writing. In Chapter 7, "Veterans Benefits: What Does the Future Hold?" we take a look at how the federal deficit impacts Veterans Benefits.

Timeline: A Look at the VA Throughout U.S. History[4]

When viewed over the course of time, the United States' policy regarding payment of federal benefits to veterans followed a pattern of growth during and after each major war.

Beginning with the Revolutionary War, military "pension" was paid to veterans seriously injured in battle and who could no longer earn a living. As the U.S. engaged in wars of longer duration and greater magnitude, "pension" expanded to provide financial aid to veterans with lesser disabilities, and to help support dependents of disabled veterans and survivors of deceased veterans.

Eventually, pensions were granted to veterans for non-service connected disabilities (injuries not resulting from military service). Finally, benefits were provided to veterans and their eligible dependents on the basis of service alone (disability not considered).

Colonial America

Benefits paid to veterans on North American soil can literally be traced back to the settlers of Plymouth Colony. As early as 1636, with Pilgrims engaged in battle with the Pequot Indians, the colony enacted a law declaring pension be paid to disabled veterans who fought in defense of the colony. Other colonies followed suit in due course.

Revolutionary War (1775–1783)

1776: The Continental Congress legislated the "original" pension law, which provided benefits in the form of pensions for disabled veterans during the Revolutionary War. If a veteran sustained loss of limb or other serious impairment, the veteran would be paid ½ pay for life. This both boosted veteran enlistments and discouraged desertion. The problem was, the Continental Congress had neither the funds nor the authority to make such payments. It was up to each state to make the actual payment to the best of its ability.

1789: The U.S. Constitution was ratified, and the first *federal* pension legislation was passed by the U.S. Congress, at that time called the Confederation Congress. The federal legislation was an extension of the pension law passed in 1776, and meant that Congress took responsibility for pensions previously paid by the states.

Pre-Civil War Era

1808: The Bureau of Pensions (under the Secretary of War) now managed all veterans programs, and soon included veterans of the War of 1812. Benefits were expanded to include widows and orphans of veterans. By 1816, the number of veterans receiving pension rose to 2,200.

1818: Congress launched the 1818 Service Pension Law. This provided the first needs-based pension, in addition to pensions awarded based on disability. Each veteran who served in the Revolutionary War and needed financial assistance would draw a fixed pension for life: $20 per month for officers and $8 per month for enlisted men.

As the 19th century progressed (and pension laws expanded), the number of veterans, eligible dependents and survivors grew to approximately 17,730. Veterans benefit payments reached $1.4 million.

1833–1858: Congress established the Bureau of Pensions in 1833. This was the first administrative body dedicated exclusively to the aid and support of veterans.

Continuing to administer Veterans Benefits, the Bureau of Pensions further evolved under various federal assignments, including the Department of War and the Navy Secretary. In 1858, the Bureau of Pensions was assigned to the new Department of the Interior.

U.S. Civil War Period (1861–1865)

During the Civil War, our nation's veterans rose in number from 80,000 to 2.4 million. Of this vast number, 600,000 veterans were killed by combat or disease, and thousands more would demand long-term care. Notably, the legacy of the Civil War encompassed the following:

- The General Pension Act of 1862, providing disability payments based on rank and degree of disability, and expanding benefits for dependents and survivors
- The establishment of the National Cemetery System
- Establishment of national medical care facilities for veterans
- Creation of the National Home for Disabled Volunteer Soldiers (NHDVS), a national government home for Union volunteer forces. By the 1920s, the level of care at the homes would rise to hospital level
- The Consolidation Act of 1873, which revised pension legislation to pay on the veteran's extent of disability rather than military rank. The Act was also the beginning of the Aid and Attendance program, at that time allowing a disabled veteran the funds to hire a nurse or home care help.

Following the Civil War, only Union veterans were eligible for federal military benefits. It wasn't until 1958 that Congress enacted reconciliatory legislation making Confederate veterans eligible for the same federal pensions as were Union veterans — thereby establishing equivalence to Union solders for service benefits.

As of August 8, 2016, a North Carolina woman — the 86-year-old daughter of a Civil War veteran — still collects his benefits.[5]

World War I (1914–1918)

1917: With U.S. engagement in the First World War, Congress put forth a new system of veterans benefits. Advancement in war technology and global locations brought exposure to new and harsh chemicals, diseases, and diverse physical and psychiatric injury. Benefit programs were opened to handle the following:

- Disability compensation
- Insurance for military personnel and veterans
- Vocational rehabilitation for disabled veterans

By 1921, the three federal agencies administering veterans benefits were:

1. The Veterans Bureau
2. The Bureau of Pensions of the Interior Department
3. The National Home for Disabled Volunteer Soldiers

Instead of a pension, any claims for veterans benefits resulting from a WWI disability or death were regarded as compensation. This designation was reversed in March 1933, when all payments to veterans were again regarded as pensions. It was not until World War II that the distinction between compensation and pension again was enforced.

1930: The Veterans Administration Is Formed

Technically, the federal agency known as the "VA" was created in 1930. Under President Herbert Hoover's order, Congress combined the three federal branches (the Veterans Bureau, the Bureau of Pensions of the Interior Department, and the National Home for Disabled Volunteer Soldiers) to establish the Veterans Administration. This consolidated all government activities affecting war veterans.

1933: The VA established the Board of Veterans Appeals. This allowed veterans to officially petition the VA's decision on a claim made for benefits (for disability, health care or cemetery) for any reason.

World War II (1941–1946)

During WWII, veterans returning after the war needed help getting back to civilian life. Hundreds of thousands of veterans came home disabled, wounded or without jobs. Countless dependents and survivors were left in need. Benefits for WWII veterans now grew to encompass health care and disability compensation for ionizing radiation exposure during military service, including various radiogenic diseases developing post-service.

Congress broadened service connected disability benefits. Congress also gave aid to the families of those veterans who were killed or disabled, before they were able to benefit from insurance.

1944 — The GI Bill of Rights

The Servicemen's Readjustment Act, more commonly known as the GI Bill of Rights, was enacted by Congress under President Roosevelt. Three essential conditions therein transformed the concept of veterans benefits, the economy and the American way of life:

1. Veterans education benefits
2. Federally guaranteed home, farm and business loans with no down payment
3. Unemployment compensation

Also in 1944, the Veteran's Preference Act was signed into law, giving veterans hiring preference in jobs funded by the federal government. This law was viable through WWII and for the following five years.

In an effort sanctioned by Congress, the Veterans Administration played a tremendous role in the development of prosthetics, assisting thousands of returning WWII amputees to receive artificial limbs and devices to support body functions. To this day, the VA's Prosthetic

& Sensory Aids Service (PSAS) is the world's most comprehensive provider of prosthetics and sensory aids.[6]

Within months following the end of WWII, the number of veterans climbed to over 15 million. VA hospitals were packed with veterans waiting in line at the 97 operating hospitals. VA increased staff to accommodate expansion in all areas of veterans benefits.

Korean War (1950–1955)

New veterans sprang from the Korean War, adding to the need for hospitals, staff and efforts by the Veterans Administration. To adjust, the VA again reorganized into three services:

1. Medical care
2. Financial assistance to veterans
3. Insurance

To handle these services, three departments were created:

1. *Department of Medicine and Surgery*
2. *Department of Veterans Benefits*
3. *Department of Insurance*

New bills were enacted to provide for unemployment insurance, job placement, home loans and more.

Vietnam War Era (1961–1975)

With the Vietnam War, the number of veterans eligible for veterans pensions grew swiftly. One important difference that arose from this war was a larger percentage of disabled veterans. There were new diseases to consider. Exposure to Agent Orange and other chemicals wrought new and devastating medical disorders. Amputations or crippling wounds were 300 percent higher than in World War II.[7]

Add to that, World War II veterans were reaching 65 years of age, meaning their age alone would qualify them as totally disabled. Disability pension benefits skyrocketed from $80 million in 1960 to $1.24 billion by 1978. The number of veterans benefit cases grew from 89,526 in 1960 to 691,045 in 1978.

Post Vietnam War

To help meet the rising cost of pensions, Congress in 1978 passed the Veterans' and Survivors' Pension Improvement Act. To calculate pension payments, previous laws did not figure in the earned income of the veteran's spouse. The new law counted all family and retirement income to determine both the veterans' eligibility for pensions and the monthly payment amount.

1979: Under Congressional order, the VA began to study the effects of Agent Orange on veterans, and, in 1983, this study was transferred to the Centers for Disease Control. The Agent Orange Act of 1991 provides for presumptive service connection for disabilities due to exposure to toxic herbicides used in the Vietnam War.

1988: The United States Court of Veterans Appeals was created. For military veterans who disagreed with a VA decision, this court gives them a chance to challenge, by judicial review, final decisions made by the VA. In 1999, this court became known as the U.S. Court of Appeals for Veterans Claims (CAVC).[8]

Veterans Administration Becomes the U.S. Department of Veterans Affairs

In 1989, under Ronald Reagan, the Department of Veterans Affairs (VA) was established, replacing the Veterans Administration. The VA is now a member of the presidential cabinet.

Gulf War (1990–present)

For VA benefit purposes, Gulf War Veterans are those men and women who served on active duty in the Southwest Asia Theater of military operations any time during the Gulf War starting August 2, 1990 through the Iraq War and subsequent reduced operations in Iraq. Military operations include Desert Shield, Desert Storm, Iraqi Freedom, and New Dawn. VA presumes certain medically unexplained symptoms and illnesses are related to Gulf War service. Eligible Veterans may receive VA disability compensation and health care benefits. Surviving spouses, dependent children and dependent parents of veterans who died as the result of illnesses related to Gulf War service may be eligible for survivors' benefits.[9]

Operation Enduring Freedom (OEF; October, 2001–December, 2014)

Veterans who served in Afghanistan during Operation Enduring Freedom (OEF) may have been exposed to a range of environmental and chemical hazards that carried potential health risks.[10]

Veterans Affairs Modernization and Reform

According to VA 2014 census data, today there are over 19 million veterans in the United States, with 1.6 million veterans living in Florida.[11] The number of Veterans receiving disability benefits in 2015 is 4.5 million.[12]

For eligible veterans and their families, the goal to reduce waiting times and increase access to medical care, and the backlog of Veterans Benefits claims and appeals, are national concerns. Efforts to reform a failed model, poor management and lack of accountability across all grade levels have been enacted and continue.

2014: Congress passed the Veterans Access, Choice and Accountability Act of 2014 (VACAA). This legislation aimed to correct problems of wait time, geographic eligibility, access to non-VA facilities, facilitate the firing of those senior VA managers with poor performance, and included funds to build new VA facilities and hire more VA doctors.

The Government Accountability Office (GAO) also has summoned the VA to implement major IT upgrades and to build capacity for managing claims workloads. The U.S. Department of Veterans Affairs undertook the mammoth task to renovate and modernize its technology and capacity. The VA has made progress and this effort is still ongoing.

While the VA has had its inglorious moments, as a veteran's advocate it is my hope that the reform that is currently underway within the VA will swiftly take hold to give veterans the first-rate service they have earned.

Current Veterans Pension and Disability Compensation Programs

Today, the Department of Veterans affairs is organized into three administrations:

1. *Veterans Benefit Administration* (VBA) — responsible for ensuring veterans get compensation, pension and other benefits, including educational benefits
2. *Veterans Health Administration* (VHA) — responsible for the VA health system
3. *National Cemetery Administration* (NCA) — responsible for administering burials and operating VA cemeteries

Through the Veterans Benefit Administration (VBA), the VA pays cash benefits of two main types to war veterans: Pension and Compensation.

1. *Pension* is paid to veterans who have minimal or no income and are disabled based on age or non-service connected disabilities.

2. *Compensation* is paid for disabilities suffered as a result of military service.

The two terms — pension and compensation — have very different meanings, and when filing a claim for veteran benefits, it is important to understand the difference. In the following chapters, we explore both service connected and non-service connected VA benefits, who is eligible for these benefits, and how to successfully file a claim for benefits from the U.S. Department of Veterans Affairs.

Chapter 2

Service Connected (SC) Veterans Benefits: Disability Compensation

Many Florida veterans, dependents and surviving spouses are entitled to service connected VA benefits. Service connected benefits are generally referred to as compensation or disability compensation.

What Is Disability Compensation?

If the veteran becomes disabled as a result of injury or disease during active service (or an existing impairment is aggravated as the result of active service causing disability), such disabilities are considered to be service connected, and the veteran is eligible for disability compensation.

The percentage of compensation is based on the veteran's disabling condition. Disability compensation benefits are tax-free and paid on a monthly basis.

What Are the Service Requirements for Compensation?

Eligibility for VA disability compensation begins with the veteran having performed active service in the U.S. military. The qualifying veteran must have sustained injuries or illness as a result of his or her active military service. Determining whether the veteran meets the active service requirement may not be a simple process. Service records will be inspected to determine

- active military service,
- where and when you served, and
- the character of your military discharge.

What Organizations Constitute "Military Service"?

By statute, a veteran is defined as a "person who served in the active military, naval or air service, and who was discharged or released therefrom under conditions other than dishonorable."[13]

However, the definition of "U.S. military" under the law may be broader than you think. Full-time active-duty service can 0mean serving with one of the five branches of the US Armed Forces:

1. US Army
2. Navy
3. Marine Corps
4. Air Force
5. Coast Guard

Other types of military service that may qualify you for VA benefits include:

- Commissioned officer of the Public Health Service

- Commissioned officer of the National Oceanic and Atmosphere Administration (NOAA)
- National Guard and Reserve Service members
- As a reserve, cadet or midshipman at a military academy
- Prior membership in Merchant Mariners or Woman's Army Auxiliary Corps (WAAC)
- In some cases, service by civilians during certain episodes of armed combat

Other organizations may exist that could lead to eligibility for VA benefits. The US Department of Veterans Affairs can be contacted for a complete list of all organizations that may qualify for veteran's benefits by calling 1-800-827-1000 or visiting their website at www.va.gov/.

Other General Requirements: Duration of Service

- The veteran must have served during a period of war (a minimum of one day).
- The veteran must have actively served 90 days or more.
- The discharge from service must be other than a "dishonorable" discharge.

What Are the Types of Discharge from Military Service?

The character of discharge a veteran needs to be eligible for either disability compensation benefits or pension benefits are the same. To receive either benefit, the veteran's character of discharge or service must be under other than dishonorable conditions (e.g., honorable discharge, and general under honorable conditions).

The following list describes all the characters of discharge authorized by the VA, and the effect each discharge has on a veteran's benefits.

Administrative Discharges

Honorable Discharge (HD) — Veterans who are honorably discharged have met or exceeded the conduct and performance standards of the U.S. military, and thus will be eligible for all VA benefits, including compensation and pension.

General Discharge (GD) Under Honorable Conditions — This character of discharge is under honorable conditions, meaning that the veteran's performance and conduct was viewed to be satisfactory. The veteran is eligible for VA benefits, including VA compensation and pension.

Other than Honorable Discharge (OTH) — An OTH discharge typically means the veteran seriously deviated from the U.S. military's expected performance and conduct. Examples include misconduct, breaches of military order, failing a drug test or drunk driving. This is an administrative discharge (as opposed to a discharges via court-martial). Qualifying for VA compensation or pension under an OTH discharge is unlikely; however, the veteran may appeal his status with the VA, where the VA examines the circumstances of the discharge to determine whether the veteran could become eligible.

Entry Level Separation — A recruit may be assigned an "uncharacterized" administrative discharge, called Entry Level Separation, for unsatisfactory performance, conduct or both. Veterans who served for less than 180 days may be granted Entry Level Separation if they could not make the grade during and immediately following basic training. A separation of this type is considered a discharge other than dishonorable. It is not Honorable or General.

Punitive Discharges

Bad Conduct Discharge (BCD) — Issued by either a special court-martial or a general court-martial, the bad conduct discharge is a punitive discharge. The question of being considered eligible for benefits depends on which military court issued the BCD. If issued by general court-marshal (the highest military court, prosecuting serious crimes) there is no further examination on the veteran's behalf. If by special court-marshal (which prosecutes crimes akin to civilian misdemeanors), the VA may investigate the circumstances to further determine the veteran's eligibility.

Dishonorable Discharge (DD) — This is the worst character of discharge, where the veteran committed a very serious crime. Examples are sexual assault and murder. The DD is dictated by a general court-martial and most likely imposed along with the maximum punishment specified in the *Manual for Courts-Martial*. Veterans receiving a Dishonorable Discharge forfeit all military and veterans benefits.

Dismissal — Dismissal is a punitive discharge much like the Bad Conduct Discharge, only imposed on officers. Special and general courts may order dismissal on officers, and is often enforced with the maximum punishment listed in the *Manual for Courts-Martial*.

Can I Upgrade a Military Discharge?

It is possible, in some cases, to upgrade a character of discharge. This is incredibly important.

It often happens that good veterans find themselves out of the military with something less than an Honorable or General Discharge. Servicemen or women may commit an offense that gets them "bad paper," and the reason is related to trauma caused by their very service. They've been to war, suffer from PTSD or depression, made a mistake, and now cannot get the VA help they desperately need.

These scenarios may lead to the tragedies of poverty, homelessness and worse. These veterans face a future with limited prospects and no VA benefits. Fortunately, there are options for these veterans. Some characterizations of discharge are eligible for recharacterization.

Each branch of service has a Discharge Review Board (DRB) that evaluates requests from veterans who want to have their character of discharge changed, corrected or upgraded. As a general rule, the characterizations eligible for consideration at the DRB are:

- General Discharge (Under Honorable Conditions),
- Other than Honorable Discharge, and
- Bad-Conduct Discharge from a Special Court-Martial.

The following forms of discharge are *not* eligible to apply to the Discharge Review Board for consideration:

- Bad-Conduct Discharge from a General Court-Martial,
- Dishonorable Discharge, or
- Dismissal.

Disability Claim Requirements

There are three main components to a claim for VA compensation. To receive disability compensation:

1. The veteran must show evidence of a current medical impairment or disabling condition;

2. There must have been some incident while on active duty that caused this condition; and

3. There must be some way to clearly link the current disabling condition to that incident. This link is called a "nexus."

How Can You Establish Service Connection?

Currently, there are five ways to establish that a disability is service connected:

1. Through direct service connection — that is, the facts, shown by evidence establish that a particular injury or disease resulting in a disability was incurred while in service in the Armed Forces;

2. Through aggravation during service — that is, a preexisting injury or disease will be considered to have been aggravated while in service in the Armed Forces;

3. Through proximity — that is, a disability which is due to, or the result of, a service connected disease or injury, which is itself considered to be service connected. An example would be a veteran developing cardiovascular disease due to a service-connected amputation of a lower limb.

4. Through a finding that the disability was caused by medical care or vocational rehabilitation provided by the Department of Veterans Affairs (VA); or

5. Through the application of statutory presumptions — that is, certain diseases as established by law or regulation are considered to have been incurred in or aggravated by service in the Armed Forces, even though there is no evidence of such disease during the period of service.[14]

Proving the connection between the event and the disabling condition can sometimes be questionable and lead to claim denial. This can delay an award of compensation, especially when the cause of injury or illness happened months or years ago. When disputes happen, you have the right to appeal the VA's denial. This involves requesting further review and reconsideration by the VA at various levels of the appeals process.

By assembling as much evidence as possible, you increase the odds that your claim is approved and the appropriate disability compensation is paid. Working with the military, as well as a physician, to put together the needed records will help ensure that, once your claim is in the VA reviewing officer's hands, it is well-documented, clear and complete.

Finally, good professional help is often the best option when establishing service connection. Counsel from a VA-accredited attorney or qualified VA representative will help ensure proper consideration of presumptive and direct theories of service connection.

How Does the VA Evaluate Levels of Disability?

Once service connection is established, the next step in the process is for the VA to rate the extent of the service connected disability. The veteran must undergo medical testing to allow the disability to be rated. The VA will evaluate the degree to which the impairment(s) affects the veteran's ability to perform work and daily activities, and the amount of benefit payment the veteran may receive. VA assesses the severity of disability based on the evidence submitted in the claim.

VA Rating Schedule

The U.S. Department of Veterans Affairs uses a rating system called the Schedule for Rating Disabilities. Ratings extend from 0% disabled to 100 percent disabled, in 10 percent increments (10 percent, 20 percent, 30 percent, etc.).

The rating schedule separates disabilities into categories based on "body systems" — the part of the body affected. Each body system category is further classified into sets of medical issues. Each set of medical issues involves specific diagnoses and diagnostic codes that identify the symptoms that qualify for varied ratings of disability.

If a disability worsens over time, it is possible for the veteran to raise his or her level of disability classification, creating a higher level of benefit payment.

Many veterans receive a rating of zero (0). This generally means the VA decided that, while the veteran's condition is service connected, it is not severe enough to call for financial compensation — according to the evidence in the claim and criteria specified in the rating schedule.

Multiple Disabilities

Veterans frequently suffer from more than one disability. In these cases, the VA calculates the disability percentage using a formula for a combined evaluation of medical criteria and disability ratings. It is important to understand that two or three individual ratings are not simply added together to produce a larger, final percentage; in fact, often only one of the ratings is chosen when the rating description matches the disability's situation most reasonably.

For example, a veteran sustained a severe back injury during a combat parachute jump — but also has type II diabetes. Both impairments are service connected. The back disorder may be given a higher disability rating because it is more representative of how the disability affects the veteran's daily life, including his or her ability to earn a living. The disability reviewer also plays a role in how the rating is determined, which adds a subjective influence to the decision.

More Than One Rating Is Possible

Secondary disabilities often materialize as a result of the primary disability. These disabilities will also need to have their own ratings. For example, if someone has a knee impairment as a result of active duty, that person might further develop arthritis, as a result, but this would get its own rating.

As years go by, injuries worsen and become more obstructing. Those who start at a 0 percent disability rating may find their rating increases over time. Having injuries reassessed will help a veteran secure the benefits owed to them because of injuries suffered as a result of active duty. One hundred percent is the total rating a veteran can have, whether there is one service connected condition or multiples.

For example: A veteran has PTSD rated at 100 percent and later develops service connected cancer, rated at 100 percent. Even though it will not increase the overall rating, the veteran should apply for the cancer compensation. The reason is that, if the PTDS rating should ever decrease, the veteran would still have 100% rating due to the service connected cancer.

Total Disability

A veteran is considered to be totally disabled when any physical or mental impairment makes it impossible for him or her to be gainfully employed again. Conditions that can be a part of total disability include:

- Loss of use of one or both hands
- Loss of use of one or both feet
- Loss of sight in both eyes
- Veteran is bedridden
- Veteran is helpless to care for himself or herself

Service Connected Benefits Are Not Needs Based

Many do not realize that the VA compensation program is not based on the veteran's economic situation. Assets, income and medical expenses are not relevant in a veteran's service connected claim. In a claim for disability compensation, only the severity of the disability and the veteran's dependents (spouse and children) factor into determining the amount of payment a veteran might receive from the VA.

100 Percent Disability Rating Warrants
Free Skilled Nursing Home Care

A 100 percent-rated veteran is entitled to free skilled nursing home care, if it is needed. (This benefit can begin at a 60 percent or higher disability rating.) This care may be provided from a VA facility or a private nursing home that contracts with the VA. The veteran would continue to be allowed to keep his or her service connected benefits. (This does not include assisted living.)

What Are Presumptive Conditions?

Certain service-related medical conditions suffered by veterans are unique to military service, under specific circumstances. Accordingly, the VA "presumes" that veterans fitting these circumstances and diseases are disabled, and compensation may be awarded. The list of presumptive diseases is extensive.

An example is a veteran who served in Vietnam between January 9, 1962 and May 7, 1975 and suffers Hodgkin's disease. That veteran would generally not have to prove nexus of evidence for the presumptive condition.

Qualifying groups of veterans include:

- Atomic veterans (exposed to ionizing radiation while on active duty)
- Vietnam veterans exposed to Agent Orange or other toxic herbicides
- Former prisoners of war (POWs)
- Gulf War veterans who have chronic disabilities (undiagnosed illness) as a result of their service
- Camp Lejeune active duty, reserve and National Guard members who served for no less than 30 days at Camp

Lejeune between August 1, 1953 and December 31, 1987

Even so, it is a good idea for the veteran to be complete and thorough, and provide detailed medical information — if, for some reason, the VA does not make the presumption allowance.

What Is Special Monthly Compensation?

A veteran who is housebound or needs assistance with activities of daily living (ADLs) due to a service connected condition can apply for additional benefits in the form of Special Monthly Compensation (SMC). The veteran would use application Form 21-526EZ and should include a doctor's letter stating the need for the SMC.

Special Monthly Compensation is paid for:[15]

- loss, or loss of use, of a hand or foot
- immobility of a joint or paralysis
- loss of sight of an eye (having only light perception)
- loss, or loss of use, of a reproductive organ
- complete loss, or loss of use, of both buttocks
- deafness of both ears (having absence of air and bone conduction)
- inability to communicate by speech (complete organic aphonea)
- loss of a percentage of tissue from a single breast, or both breasts, from mastectomy or radiation treatment

For a veteran who is already receiving compensation, SMC is in addition to it. If the veteran is either housebound or requires assistance with ADLs, Special Monthly Compensation may also be paid for Aid and Attendance (A&A).

What Is Combat-Related Special Compensation?

Retired military veterans with conditions related to combat should apply for Combat-Related Special Compensation (CRSC) from the Department of Defense (DOD). This payment is distributed in addition to the veteran's retirement pay and their VA disability compensation. However, certain criteria must be met before the veteran can receive CRSC payments:

- The veteran must also be receiving (or be entitled to receive) military retired pay.
- The veteran must be medically retired with 20 years of credible service.
- The VA injury must be rated 10 percent or higher.

These special compensation benefits are applied for in addition to other benefits that come along with service connected disabilities.

Compensation Benefit Rates: What VA Disability Benefits Look Like With and Without Dependents

The figures for the service connected disability benefits will fluctuate, based on the number of dependents the veteran might have. The more dependents who are present, the higher the benefits, in addition to having a higher benefit when the disability rating is higher.

The VA compensation rates for those veterans with a disability rating of over 10 percent, updated for 2017 (effective as of December 1, 2016) are:[16]

With or Without Dependents (monthly benefits)
Disability rating of 10% = $133.57
Disability rating of 20% = $264.02

For Those Without Dependents

—30 to 60 Percent Disability Rating—

Without Dependents (monthly benefits), Veteran Alone
Disability rating of 30% = $408.97
Disability rating of 40% = $589.12
Disability rating of 50% = $838.64
Disability rating of 60% = $1,062.27

Without Dependents (monthly benefits), Veteran with Spouse
Disability rating of 30% = $456.97
Disability rating of 40% = $654.12
Disability rating of 50% = $919.64
Disability rating of 60% = $1,159.27

Without Dependents (monthly benefits), Veteran, Spouse and One Parent
Disability rating of 30% = $495.97
Disability rating of 40% = $706.12
Disability rating of 50% = $984.64
Disability rating of 60% = $1,237.27

Without Dependents (monthly benefits), Veteran, Spouse and Two Parents
Disability rating of 30% = $534.97
Disability rating of 40% = $758.12
Disability rating of 50% = $1,049.64
Disability rating of 60% = $1,315.27

Without Dependents (monthly benefits), Veteran and One Parent
Disability rating of 30% = $447.97
Disability rating of 40% = $641.12
Disability rating of 50% = $903.64
Disability rating of 60% = $1,140.27

Without Dependents (monthly benefits), Veteran with Two Parents
Disability rating of 30% = $486.97
Disability rating of 40% = $693.12
Disability rating of 50% = $968.64
Disability rating of 60% = $1,218.27

Without Dependents, Additional Compensation for Spouse Who Needs Assistance
Disability rating of 30% = $45.00
Disability rating of 40% = $59.00
Disability rating of 50% = $74.00
Disability rating of 60% = $89.00

—70 to 100 Percent Disability Rating—

Without Dependents (monthly benefits), Veteran Alone
Disability rating of 70% = $1,338.71
Disability rating of 80% = $1,556.13
Disability rating of 90% = $1,748.71
Disability rating of 100% = $2,915.55

Without Dependents (monthly benefits), Veteran with Spouse
Disability rating of 70% = $1,451.71
Disability rating of 80% = $1,686.13
Disability rating of 90% = $1,894.71
Disability rating of 100% = $3,078.11

Without Dependents (monthly benefits), Veteran, Spouse and One Parent

Disability rating of 70% = $1,542.71
Disability rating of 80% = $1,790.13
Disability rating of 90% = $2,011.71
Disability rating of 100% = $3,208.56

Without Dependents (monthly benefits), Veteran, Spouse and Two Parents

Disability rating of 70% = $1,633.71
Disability rating of 80% = $1,894.13
Disability rating of 90% = $2,128.71
Disability rating of 100% = $3,339.01

Without Dependents (monthly benefits), Veteran and One Parent

Disability rating of 70% = $1,429.71
Disability rating of 80% = $1,660.13
Disability rating of 90% = $1,865.71
Disability rating of 100% = $3,046.00

Without Dependents (monthly benefits), Veteran with Two Parents

Disability rating of 70% = $1,520.71
Disability rating of 80% = $1,764.13
Disability rating of 90% = $1,982.71
Disability rating of 100% = $3,176.45

Additional Compensation for Spouse Who Needs Assistance

Disability rating of 70% = $105.00
Disability rating of 80% = $119.00
Disability rating of 90% = $134.00
Disability rating of 100% = $149.08

For Those With Dependents

—30 to 60% Disability Rating—

With Dependents (monthly benefits), Veteran, Spouse and Child
Disability rating of 30% = $492.97
Disability rating of 40% = $702.12
Disability rating of 50% = $978.64
Disability rating of 60% = $1,230.27

With Dependents (monthly benefits), Veteran with Child Only
Disability rating of 30% = $440.97
Disability rating of 40% = $632.12
Disability rating of 50% = $892.64
Disability rating of 60% = $1,127.27

With Dependents (monthly benefits), Veteran, Spouse, One Parent and Child
Disability rating of 30% = $531.97
Disability rating of 40% = $754.12
Disability rating of 50% = $1,043.64
Disability rating of 60% = $1,308.27

With Dependents (monthly benefits), Veteran, Spouse, Two Parents and Child
Disability rating of 30% = $570.97
Disability rating of 40% = $806.12
Disability rating of 50% = $1,108.64
Disability rating of 60% = $1,386.27

With Dependents (monthly benefits), Veteran with One Parent and Child
Disability rating of 30% = $479.97
Disability rating of 40% = $684.12
Disability rating of 50% = $957.64
Disability rating of 60% = $1,205.27

With Dependents (monthly benefits), Veteran with Two Parents and Child
Disability rating of 30% = $518.97
Disability rating of 40% = $736.12
Disability rating of 50% = $1,022.64
Disability rating of 60% = $1,283.27

Add for Each Additional Child Under 18
Disability rating of 30% = $24.00
Disability rating of 40% = $32.00
Disability rating of 50% = $40.00
Disability rating of 60% = $48.00

Add for Each Additional Child Over 18 Who is Attending School
Disability rating of 30% = $78.00
Disability rating of 40% = $104.00
Disability rating of 50% = $130.00
Disability rating of 60% = $156.00

Additional Compensation for Spouse Who Needs Assistance
Disability rating of 30% = $45.00
Disability rating of 40% = $59.00
Disability rating of 50% = $74.00
Disability rating of 60% = $89.00

—70 to 100 Percent Disability Rating—

With Dependents (monthly benefits), Veteran, Spouse and Child
Disability rating of 70% = $1,534.71
Disability rating of 80% = $1,781.13
Disability rating of 90% = $2,001.71
Disability rating of 100% = $3,197.16

With Dependents (monthly benefits), Veteran with Child Only
Disability rating of 70% = $1,414.71
Disability rating of 80% = $1,642.13
Disability rating of 90% = $1,845.71
Disability rating of 100% = $3,024.27

With Dependents (monthly benefits), Veteran, Spouse, One Parent and Child
   Disability rating of 70% = $1,625.71
   Disability rating of 80% = $1,885.13
   Disability rating of 90% = $2,118.71
   Disability rating of 100% = $3,327.61

With Dependents (monthly benefits), Veteran, Spouse, Two Parents and Child
   Disability rating of 70% = $1,716.71
   Disability rating of 80% = $1,989.13
   Disability rating of 90% = $2,235.71
   Disability rating of 100% = $3,458.06

With Dependents (monthly benefits), Veteran with One Parent and Child
   Disability rating of 70% = $1,505.71
   Disability rating of 80% = $1,746.13
   Disability rating of 90% = $1,962.71
   Disability rating of 100% = $3,154.72

With Dependents (monthly benefits), Veteran with Two Parents and Child
   Disability rating of 70% = $1,596.71
   Disability rating of 80% = $1,850.13
   Disability rating of 90% = $2,079.71
   Disability rating of 100% = $3,285.17

Add for Each Additional Child Under 18
   Disability rating of 70% = $56.00
   Disability rating of 80% = $64.00
   Disability rating of 90% = $72.00
   Disability rating of 100% = $80.76

Add for Each Additional Child Over 18 Who is Attending School
Disability rating of 70% = $182.00
Disability rating of 80% = $208.00
Disability rating of 90% = $234.00
Disability rating of 100% = $260.91
Additional Compensation for Spouse Who Needs Assistance
Disability rating of 70% = $105.00
Disability rating of 80% = $119.00
Disability rating of 90% = $134.00
Disability rating of 100% = $149.08

Other Service Connected Benefits

Veterans are able to receive more than just monthly payments. You may also automatically qualify for various benefits if you meet certain conditions and disability ratings. The following list, while not complete, outlines some key service connected benefits available that can prove to be quite beneficial:

Long-Term Care

Nursing home care is covered for veterans in need of nursing home care for a service related injury, condition or disease.

- Veterans who are 60 percent service connected disabled or higher, and who cannot work, qualify for unlimited nursing home care.

- Veterans who are 70 percent service connected disabled or higher qualify for unlimited nursing home care.

Co-Payments

Veterans seeking care for a service connected disability do not have to pay a co-payment on medical visits pertaining to that condition.

Prescriptions

- Veterans who are 50 percent service connected disabled or higher do not have to pay for prescriptions.
- Veterans who use a medication for a service connected disability do not have to pay for medication.

Life Insurance

Service connected disabled veterans are able to retain life insurance policies as a part of their benefits and may also be able to apply for additional disabled veteran's insurance, which has low rates. Part of the eligibility requirements are that the veteran should apply within two years from the date VA grants the new service connected disability compensation.

Disabled Transition Assistance Program (DTAP)

What happens when a veteran's time in the military ends due to disability and he or she must reenter civilian life? The Disabled Transition Assistance Program provides guidance to veterans who are leaving military service with a service connected disability, and veterans who have a VA rating of 10 percent plus and will be filing claims with the VA.

The DTAP provides group presentations and discussions about the VA's Vocational Rehabilitation and Employment (VR&E) program. Veterans learn whether they qualify for assistance through the VR&E, and the program provides opportunities for the veteran to fill out an application for vocational rehabilitation benefits.

Through DTAP, veterans decide whether this program applies to their lives. Sessions can be coordinated to accommodate those veterans who might be in the hospital, an assisted living facility or are simply unable to go to one of the sessions. Veterans bring their medical records to help them review their case with trained professionals.

Dependency and Indemnity Compensation (DIC)

Dependency and Indemnity Compensation (DIC) is a monthly benefit paid to eligible survivors of veterans. These are veterans who died while on active duty or whose death after service resulted from a service connected injury or disease. DIC is also paid as the result of improper treatment of the deceased veteran from the VA health care or rehabilitation services. DIC is automatically granted to a surviving spouse for a veteran who was permanently and totally disabled for 10 years or more. This is a tax-free benefit.

Service Connected Benefits by Disability Rating[17]

Quite a few VA benefits are possible when a service connected disability has been determined. Knowing what you might be able to benefit from will allow you not only to save money but also to have peace of mind for yourself and for your family.

0 Percent and Higher

- Home Loan Guaranty Certificate of Eligibility
- $10,000 Life Insurance Policy — Veterans must file within the two-year span of filing for their service connected disability
- Outpatient treatment for conditions related to service injuries
- Travel allowance to VA facilities for scheduled appointments for service connected conditions (based on income level or 25+ miles distance traveled from home)
- Medical treatment for any condition, if enrolled in VA health care program
- VA doctor-prescribed prosthetic devices, including tanks

of oxygen, wheelchairs, nebulizers, canes, crutches, hospital beds, motorized scooters and other related equipment, depending on the circumstance

- Medical treatment with VA issued and authorized fee-basis card in non-VA facilities for service connected conditions
- Civil Service Preference — Ten (10) points added to a Civil Service test score if 70 or higher score obtained by the veteran
- Yearly clothing allowance of $779.62 for veterans with a service connected condition requiring the use of a VA prescribed prosthetic appliance or who use VA prescribed medications for a skin condition that wears or soils articles of clothing
- Temporary 100 percent rating when hospitalized for a service connected disability. This rating requires at least one month of immobilization by cast and/or recuperation
- Dental treatment or follow-up treatment for a service connected condition. Former POWs with 90+ consecutive days of confinement also receive this treatment
- Home Improvement and Structural Alterations (HISA) Grant Program — Service connected veterans can receive a lifetime HISA benefit up to $6,800, while non-service connected veterans may receive a lifetime HISA benefit up to $2,000 for improving their homes to provide accessibility for injuries and disabilities

10 Percent and Higher, *all of the above, plus*:

- Vocational rehabilitation which includes full medical and dental care, and allowance (as well as disability payments), payment for all school-related supplies which are required by the program and tuition payments to the school
- Home loan guaranty loans will not require funding fee

30 Percent and Higher, *all of the above, plus*:

- Additional monetary compensation for dependents
- Job appointment without an interview to civil service position
- Employment affirmation action
- Additional allowance for a spouse in long-term care facility

40 Percent and Higher, *all of the above, plus*:

- One time automobile grant of up to $20,235.20. Veteran must have a service connected loss, or permanent loss of use, of one or both feet, or the loss, or permanent loss of use, of one or both hands, or permanent impairment of vision in both eyes to a certain degree, or severe burn injury, or Amyotrophic Lateral Sclerosis (ALS)[18]
- Payment for adaptive devices for the automobile related to disability

50 Percent and Higher, *all of the above, plus*:

- $0 co-payment for treatment of non-service connected care or prescription drugs
- Medical treatment with fee-basis card in non-VA facilities for any condition

60–90 Percent and Higher, *all of the above, plus*:

- Increased compensation for veteran, payable at the 100% rate, if unable to work due to service connected disability

100 Percent or Complete Loss of Employability, *all of the above, plus*:

- Unlimited dental treatment
- Educational funding for dependents — some restrictions apply
- CHAMPVA benefits — Health and medical program for survivors and dependents

- Grants up to 50% of a home's cost (no more than $67,555) for building, purchasing or remodeling homes to be supportive of disabilities. These grants can also help to pay toward a balance on an existing home mortgage[19]
- Grants up to $13,511 to assist in adapting a veteran's home or to acquire a new or previously owned residence which is already adapted for the disability[20]
- Veteran's Mortgage Life Insurance (VMLI) — Decreasing term mortgage insurance up to $200,000 for veterans who have received a Specially Adaptive Housing grant and who already have an existing mortgage[21]
- Waiver of cost of life insurance
- Additional $10,000 of life insurance
- Commissary privileges for veteran and dependents of disabled veteran
- Exchange privileges for veterans and dependents of disabled veteran
- Emergency treatment in non-VA facilities if VA facilities are unavailable
- Yearly eye exams and prescribed eye wear
- Special compensation, based on disability ratings and other special situations

How to Apply for Service Connected Disability Benefits

For veterans who need to submit claims for disability compensation (and for dual pension and compensation claims), VA has initiated Centralized Mail processing (CM). This allows disabled veteran claimants or beneficiaries to send all mail directly to the

Jainesville, Wisconsin Intake Center. Mail to:

Department of Veterans Affairs
Claims Intake Center
PO Box 4444
Janesville, WI 53547-4444

Or Fax to:

TOLL FREE: 844-531-7818
248-524-4260 (Utilized for Foreign claimants)

Central Mail processing is part of the VA's efforts to expedite claims processing. The process transforms decentralized mail intake at the Regional Offices (RO) to a more efficient centralized process. VBA still receives mail from a variety of sources in various formats and methods — meaning incoming mail is handled multiple times before it can be processed. CM reduces processing time, increases mail monitoring and improves timeliness of claims establishment.

**The VA Still Offers Various Ways
to Apply for VA Compensation:**

- *eBenefits*: Apply online using an eBenefits account. Go to www.ebenefits.va.gov/ebenefits/homepage
- *Centralized Mail processing*: Complete and mail (or fax) your claim form to the Janesville, WI Claims Intake Center
- *Regional Office*: Complete and mail your claim form to your nearest VA regional office (who will then forward the claim to the Janesville, WI Claims Intake Center)
- *Fully Developed Claim* (FDC): Fast track your claim review by submitting a "Fully Developed Claim" (as explained further in this chapter)
- *Work with an accredited VA Attorney or Agent* (see Chapter 6)
- *Go to a VA Regional Office* where people are on staff

to help you navigate the process. To find the VA regional office nearest you, visit www.va.gov/directory/guide/ home.asp or call VA toll free at 1-800-827-1000. The services are free and the paperwork can be sent directly to your physician or therapist for further documentation.

In all cases, when filing your claim it is critical to understand what evidence the VA requires, and that you know what is your responsibility, and what is the responsibility of the VA.

Veterans Records Destroyed by Fire in 1973

On July 12, 1973, a fire at the National Personnel Records Center (NPRC) in St. Louis destroyed records held for veterans who were discharged from the Army and Air Force.

The fire destroyed 80 percent of the records held for veterans who were discharged from the Army between November 1, 1912 and January 1, 1960.

The fire destroyed 75 percent of the records held for veterans who were discharged from the Air Force between September 25, 1947 and January 1, 1964, with surnames beginning with Hubbard and running through the end of the alphabet.[22]

How a Veteran Can Prove Service In Spite of Destroyed Records

Veterans filing a claim whose records were destroyed in the fire can take the following actions:

- Submit NA Form 13055, "Request for Information Needed to Reconstruct Medical Data" with your claim. VA will use the form as their request to the NPRC to do more research or reconstruct any applicable records.

- Contact the court house records department in the county where the veteran lived at the time of discharge. Many of these court houses contain original discharge documents.
- If there is a buddy who will sign an affidavit that would help prove active duty during war time, such an affidavit may be sufficient.
- Contact the Defense Finance and Accounting Service to have them send pay vouchers or history of payment while in service. That, along with the copy of the discharge papers, should be enough for the archives to release a certificate of active duty.

Duty to Assist

Decisions concerning VA benefit eligibility and entitlement are based on the evidence of record. Evidence includes documents, records, testimonials and other information that support the veteran's claim for benefits.

Before making a final decision, VA has a "duty to assist" the veteran in locating and gathering essential and supporting evidence to complete the claim. This may include the following relevant federal records:

- VA medical records,
- service medical records,
- Social Security Administration records, or
- evidence from other federal agencies.

And the following relevant non-federal records:

- private medical records
- lay or other non-federal governmental evidence, such as employer records or state and local government records.

If an examination or a medical opinion is necessary to make a decision on a claim for compensation, then VA's duty to assist often includes:

- examining claimants, and/or
- obtaining a medical opinion from the Veterans Health Administration (VHA) or designated contracted provider.

Fully Developed Claims (FDC) Program — Disability Compensation

The FDC program is an optional new approach that offers veterans, service members and survivors faster decisions from the VA on benefit claims. Applications for Veterans Disability Compensation and Dependency and Indemnity Compensation (DIC) may use the Fully Developed Claim process.

VA recommends filing the Fully Developed Claim online at www. eBenefits.va.gov. At the time the veteran makes the claim, he or she must:

- submit all required records and every shred of evidence and documentation, as completely as possible, including federal, non-federal and medical records, and
- certify that he or she has no further evidence to submit.

The burden is on the veteran to provide the essential information up front. Once the application is submitted, the veteran waives his or her rights to the VA's duty to assist in obtaining evidence. The veteran also forfeits the option to add further evidence to support the claim.

For the FDC program, the VA will only obtain service treatment records and federal treatment records when they are identified. If necessary, the VA will also send the veteran for a VA medical exam.

The goal is to have the claim reviewed and decided faster, within months, rather than waiting up to 18 months using the traditional claim filing and review process.

What Records Are Needed?

Military personnel records: Certified copy or original discharge papers. Since January 1, 1950, the separation form issued is the DD Form 214. Before January 1, 1950, several similar forms were used by the military services, including the WD AGO 53, WD AGO 55, WD AGO 53-55, NAVPERS 553, NAVMC 78PD, and the NAVCG 553. Use the Standard Form 180 (SF 180) to request military records from the National Personnel Records Center (NPRC).

Military personnel records may also include deployment orders, pay records, medals and certificates not reflected on the DD 214.

Military treatment records: Medical evidence of a current physical or mental disability including a log of any conditions or injuries you suffered in service — and — evidence of a link between your current disability and the event, injury or disease in military service. Medical records or medical opinions are usually required to establish this relationship.

Other federal records: such as from Social Security Administration (SSA) which may contain medical evidence or even evidence as to the cause of a disability.

Non-federal records: such as medical files from your private doctor which may inform as to the degree of your condition, if it has worsened over time, or other data to assist rating purposes.

The Fully Developed Claim process may also be used to:

- Reopen a currently filed disability claim that the VA could not grant (and is over one year old)
- Claim for increased disability
- Claim for Secondary disability

Remember: With the Fully Developed Claim process, you surrender your rights to VA assistance or further admission to the claim. To ensure nothing is missed and no mistakes are made, it a good idea to appoint an accredited attorney, representative or agent to assist you in developing and completing the submission.

What If the Fully Developed Claim Is Found to Be Deficient or Incomplete?

The VA promotes the FDC program as a "no risk" program. If VA finds that key records are missing and should be included before the claim can be decided, VA would take the claim out of the FDC program and process it through the traditional claims process.

You have up to one year to complete your claim once the FDC process begins. If your claim is approved, benefits would be paid retroactively to the day your claim was begun.

Chapter 3

Non-Service Connected (NSC) Veterans Benefit: Pension

While some veterans are compensated for disabilities sustained as a result of military service, other veterans may receive a VA benefit called Pension. Both Veterans Pension and Survivors Pension benefits provide supplemental income to eligible low-income veterans and their surviving spouses (and certain dependent children) to help them manage costs associated with aging, disability and illness, and general costs of living. Pension benefits are tax free. The monthly benefit amount is based on the veteran's or survivor's family income. Hence, VA Pension is needs based, whereas Disability Compensation benefits are based on service connected disability.

As a senior or disabled veteran, you may be overwhelmed with the tremendous expenses involved with assisted living facilities or skilled nursing home care, or various forms of in-home care. For veterans who are low income, served during wartime and are either totally disabled or have reached age 65, a solution to help pay for long-term care may be sought through the Veterans Pension program. As Florida's veteran population ages, it is vital that military families learn about and apply for this important benefit available to them from the VA.

What Is Veterans Pension?

The Department of Veterans Affairs offers three levels of pension benefits:

1. Basic monthly pension
2. Housebound
3. Aid and Attendance

Monthly Pension

Veterans Pension is a monthly payment intended to help qualifying wartime veterans with limited income. Many veterans are uninformed of the fact that, if they are 65 or older and on a limited income, they may qualify for a VA Pension, even if they are in good health.

Surviving spouses, and certain dependents of eligible wartime veterans, who meet both the asset and net-worth requirements, may qualify for a monthly pension known as Survivors Pension (formerly called Death Pension).

Benefits Paid In Addition to Monthly Pension

In many cases, veterans need help paying for medical expenses associated with illness or disabilities that are not related to their military service. Veterans and survivors who qualify for basic, monthly VA Pension, also may suffer health issues to the point they are considered housebound or require the aid and attendance of another person.

These individuals would qualify for additional monetary allowances known as Aid and Attendance (A&A) and/or Housebound benefits. These additional benefits are specifically designed to help veterans pay expenses associated with being confined to their home and/or requiring an assisted living setting or nursing home care due to their disability.

Veterans in need of Aid and Attendance or Housebound assistance often find their income is too high to meet the income and asset limits required for basic pension. The good news is that households with higher incomes still may qualify for Aid and Attendance and Housebound benefits through medical deductions and other means.

Many veterans are not fully aware of these significant benefits or do not realize they are eligible for them. We will examine all applicable scenarios in the following pages.

Who Qualifies for Non-Service Connected Pension Benefits?

The veteran must meet eligibility requirements for age or disability, military service and financial need. First, we'll look at the non-financial requirements regarding disability and age, service and periods of wartime, and the allowable types of discharge from service.

Non-Financial Requirements for VA Pension Eligibility

- *Age/Disability*: Veterans must have served during a period of war, must be at least 65 years of age, or have a permanent and total non-service connected disability if younger.

- *A veteran who has attained age 65* does not need to be disabled to qualify for pension at the basic monthly rate.

- *A veteran who is a patient in a nursing home or is receiving Social Security Disability benefits* is considered permanently and totally disabled by VA and may qualify for additional monetary payments, known as Aid and Attendance and Housebound allowances.

- *Survivors*: There are no disability or age criteria for a surviving spouse. The individual must be an un-remarried, low-income, surviving spouse of a deceased wartime veteran. A surviving child must be under the age of 18, or under the age of 23 and attending a VA-approved school, or incapable of supporting his or herself due to a disability.

- *Military Service*: Veterans must be considered "wartime veterans." This means they served at least 90 days total and served at least 1 day during a wartime date as established by U.S. Congress. (Wartime dates are listed in this chapter.)

- The veteran need not to have engaged in combat.

- In addition, veterans who enlisted after September 7, 1980 will need to have served for at least 24 months in total or completed his or her entire tour of active duty, i.e. National Reserves and/or the National Guard.

- Character of Discharge: The veteran's discharge status must be under "other than dishonorable" conditions. As a general rule, this means Honorable Discharge or General Discharge.

Wartime Dates for Non-Service Connected Veterans Pension

- World War II: December 7, 1941—December 31, 1946
- Korean Conflict: June 27, 1950—January 31, 1955
- Vietnam Era: February 28, 1961—May 7, 1975 (If service was in the Republic of Vietnam)
- Vietnam Era: August 5, 1964—May 7, 1975 (If service was not in the Republic of Vietnam)
- Persian Gulf War: August 2, 1990—Continuing

Income Requirements for VA Pension

As an income-based program, veterans and their survivors must meet economic limitations to be eligible for Veterans Pension. You must have low or no countable income and meet the net worth/asset limitations.

First, we need to understand three terms: MAPR, UME and IVAP:

1. *Maximum Annual Pension Rate* (MAPR): As a needs-based benefit, pension is based on the veteran's maximum permissible yearly income. This is called the Maximum Annual Pension Rate (MAPR).

2. *Unreimbursed Medical Expenses* (UME): For both A&A and Housebound pension benefits, VA will reimburse recurring medical expenses for which a veteran pays out of pocket. These expenses are generally those that recur each month, starting from the date of the application going forward for the future 12-month period. The unreimbursed expenses must exceed 5 percent of the applicable MAPR. (This is also called the "5 percent deductible.")

3. *Income for VA Purposes* (IVAP): This is the applicant's household income, minus all unreimbursed medical expenses (UMEs). The Pension benefit dollar amount is the difference between the MAPR and the veteran's gross household income, after deducting recurring medical expenses. To be deducted, medical expenses must exceed 5 percent of MAPR. The adjusted income is what the VA calls "Income for VA Purposes" or IVAP.

The Income Test

To qualify for pension at the Basic, Housebound and Aid and Attendance levels, the veteran must meet the following financial criteria:

- *Income*: A veteran's countable family income (both

husband and wife, if both are living) must be less than the yearly limit (MAPR) to qualify for a benefit. Income is what a veteran or their surviving spouse might receive in a year, after deducting health care and medical expenses. The surviving family is not eligible for Survivors Pension if their circumstances change and their household income exceeds the limit set by Congress.

- *Net Worth/Assets*: The VA wants to know whether a claimant should use some portion of his or her own resources before he or she is granted needs-based benefits. Therefore, a large "net worth" might affect a veteran's eligibility. To meet VA Pension's needs-based intent, a veteran should not have assets that could support him or her financially for a long time, as determined by the VA. "Net worth" signifies the value of all your assets that can be converted into money — bank accounts, stocks, bonds, CDs, mutual funds and real estate — other than your home. There is no dollar asset limit set forth by law, however. The determination of eligibility can be made at the discretion of a VA caseworker. You should contact a VA accredited attorney if you have financial assets exceeding $30,000, outside of your house and your car.

Can I Transfer Assets to Meet VA Pension Limits?

You or your spouse may have assets that put your household over VA's permissible financial limit. As of this 2017 writing, transfers of assets for the purpose of reducing a veteran's countable income are allowed by VA. For example, if you transfer

$35,000 to your son and a week later apply for VA Pension, the $35,000 transfer is acceptable and legal.*

How Are Countable Income and Net Worth Determined?

To qualify for the Veterans Pension benefit, your annual family income must be below the Maximum Annual Pension Rate (MAPR). This rate is the yearly limit set by Congress. You will see how MAPR affects the Basic, Housebound, and Aid and Attendance benefit amounts in tables later in this chapter.

Your pension benefit is the difference between your "countable" income and the MAPR. VA generally pays this difference in 12 equal monthly payments.

Countable income includes gross family income from most sources. So, exactly what income is "countable" for Veterans Pension eligibility purposes?

Countable Income

Countable income is defined as income that a veteran or their surviving spouse might receive in a year, after health care costs are deducted.

As mentioned earlier, the household income cannot exceed the MAPR for your pension income category. Some expenses, such as unreimbursed medical expenses, may also reduce your countable income. If your income is over the MAPR, you may be able to show that your medical expenses reduce your monthly income to the point that you qualify.

---

*Alert! VA has proposed a rule that will establish a look-back period for asset transfers. Once the proposed rule becomes law, many VA Pension asset and income rules will change. Please see Chapter 7, "Veterans Benefits: What Does the Future Hold?" for important information about how this will make qualifying for long-term care more difficult for veterans; as veterans will lose an asset planning opportunity.

What "countable income" includes:

- Income from most sources (including Social Security and including that of eligible dependents)
- Checking and savings accounts
- IRAs, CDs, interest and dividend payments from annuities, stocks, bonds, pension, military Survivor Benefit Plan (SBP) annuity, etc.
- Disability payments
- Assets owned by the spouse
- Net income from farming or other home business

What "countable income" does not include:

- Primary residence or vehicle
- Life insurance policies with no cash value
- SSI — Supplemental Security Income
- Food stamps
- Welfare benefits

Net Worth/Assets

Net worth is about market value. In assessing net worth, the VA considers U.S. and overseas bank accounts, stocks, bonds, mutual funds, annuities, and certain real and personal property owned by the veteran and/or spouse. Items that are NOT counted toward a claimant's net worth are: the primary residence and lot, a vehicle used for the claimant's care, household goods and personal effects (such as furniture, clothes, jewelry, art).

Some assets can be counted as income. Many do not realize that the VA will consider certain assets and investments, which can be easily converted to money, to be part of their "countable income." This can put some veterans over the MAPR, even if their annual income does not.

There are no set dollar limits for the VA caseworker to follow when assigning the individual's net worth. While "ballpark estimates" of

$80,000 for a couple and $40,000 for an individual are often cited, various levels of assets could possibly prevent an award. VA caseworkers must use a certain amount of judgment in establishing the household's net worth.

Basically, the VA's determination should gauge whether your assets are of a sufficiently large amount that you could live off of them for a reasonable period of time — as opposed to having financial need for VA Pension payments.

Unreimbursed Medical Expenses (UME) — How They Help You Meet VA Income Limits

A disabled veteran, or widow of a deceased veteran, may earn a higher annual income than permitted under the desired pension's Maximum Annual Pension Rate (MAPR). This is when the Unreimbursed Medical Expense (UME) provision may be of great help, as UME's offset countable income.

Many veterans, or spouses of veterans, have recurring medical expenses that they pay for themselves. The VA considers these as "Unreimbursed Medical Expenses" that the VA can deduct when they calculate the claimant's countable income. These significant deductions often allow a disabled veteran's household with "too much income" to meet the VA's income and asset limits.

The scope of UME is rather broad, and may include the costs of:

- nursing home fees
- assisted living facility
- in-home care
- adult day care
- home modifications to accommodate elderly needs or disabilities

- Medicare insurance premiums
- prosthetics
- medical equipment, certain medicines and prescription drugs, and various other supplies

One recurring medical expense that may *not* be allowed as a UME is that of prescription drugs. For instance, a veteran may spend $400 monthly out-of-pocket for a prescription drug that is required. While it may be difficult to have medications allowed prospectively, it is not impossible. You may be successful through working with your treating doctor, to document and support the necessity of the medication, and with your pharmacy, to provide history of use and expense for the VA to allow it. There has been success in these efforts.

As a general rule, unreimbursed medical expenses that exceed 5 percent of the MAPR are deductible.

The deduction of Unreimbursed Medical Expenses can be of tremendous aid to the veteran's household, as these will decrease the countable income and increase monthly pension entitlements. Even if a veteran's income is over the MAPR, certain expenses may put the "countable income" within range of eligibility.

For example, a veteran and spouse earning $4,500 a month could still qualify for Aid and Attendance if the veteran is spending $4,100 a month on home health service expenses, medical equipment rentals and monthly Medicare deductions.

UME can help qualify veterans with incomes over the MAPR, who are current residents in an assisted living facility or a nursing home, to receive Aid and Attendance. The monthly payments from A&A will help to pay the cost of the assisted living facility or skilled nursing home. Consequently, Aid and Attendance benefits can sometimes eliminate the need to apply for Medicaid — for some assisted living residents.

UME is a key component to becoming eligible for Aid and

Attendance and Housebound benefits. Sadly, many veterans and their spouses are not aware of this provision, and, consequently, only a fraction of eligible military households are actually receiving pension.

The Three Levels of Veterans Pension

As a veteran, you may be eligible for different levels of VA Pension: Basic Level, and two types of enhanced pension: Housebound, and Aid and Attendance (A&A).

When you (or a survivor) need medical assistance or supervision due to disability, the VA will rate you as being housebound, or rate you as needing the regular aid and attendance of another person.

If you do not need Aid and Attendance or Housebound benefits, the Maximum Annual Pension Rate (MAPR) will be quite low. By contrast, the MAPR is much higher for a veteran or survivor seeking Aid and Attendance or Housebound medical ratings.

Basic Pension Level

This is the "ground level" of VA Pension, because there is no qualification regarding the veteran's health care needs. Basic pension is for able-bodied veterans with very low incomes. Eligibility includes meeting the financial limitations, plus, the claimant must have served during a time of war, be at minimum 65 years old, unemployed, with an "other than dishonorable" discharge.

The following table shows the VA's 2017 Maximum Annual Pension Rates (MAPR) available for basic pension. Benefits became effective December 1, 2016 and include a 0.3% Cost-of-Living Increase, effective December 1, 2016.

Household Status	Basic Pension MAPR	Medical Deduction: Expenses must exceed 5% of MAPR or:
A veteran alone	Up to $12,907/year	$645
A veteran + one dependent	Up to $16,902/year	$845
Surviving spouse	Up to $8,656	$432
Surviving spouse + one dependent	Up to $11,330	$566
Two veterans married to one another	Up to $16,902/year	$845
Each additional dependent child	Add $ 2,205/year	—

As an income-only based pension, there is no medical rating; there may be recurring medical expenses to be calculated in the IVAP, such as insurance or Medicare premiums.

Example:

Jerry, a resident of Bradford County, Florida is a single 68-year-old Vietnam veteran. His is in good physical and mental health, yet he is struggling to get by. Jerry applies for the basic VA Pension.

Gross Income: His only income is Social Security retirement, which is $910 a month, or $10,920 a year.

Medical Expenses: Jerry pays $1,200 a year for Medicare Part B, which the VA recognizes as an unreimbursed medical expense (UME).

Adjusted Medical Expense: As required by law, the VA will adjust Jerry's medical expenses with the 5 percent deduction, or $645: $1,200 − $645 = $555 per year.

IVAP: Next, the VA will determine Jerry's IVAP (Income for VA Purposes), which is his household (gross) income minus the adjusted unreimbursed medical expenses (UMEs) $10,920 – $555 = $10,365 (IVAP).

To determine the Pension amount, the VA will subtract Jerry's IVAP ($10,365) from the basic Pension MAPR for a single veteran ($12,907): $12,907 – $10,365 = $2,542.

VA awards Jerry a yearly pension amount of $2,542, or approximately $211.83 a month.

Housebound Level

Housebound allowance is a higher rate of VA Pension for veterans or surviving spouses who qualify for basic pension and who are confined to his or her home due to permanent disability. To receive a "housebound" medical rating and before benefits will be dispensed, veterans will need to have their condition verified by their treating physician and in accordance with VA medical standards.

Below are the VA's 2017 Maximum Annual Pension Rates (MAPR) available for housebound allowances. Benefits became effective December 1, 2016 and include a 0.3% Cost-of-Living Increase effective December 1, 2016.

Household Status	Housebound MAPR	Medical Deduction: Expenses must exceed 5% of MAPR or:
A veteran alone	$15,773 / year	$645
A veteran + one dependent	$19,770 / year	$845
Each additional dependent child	Add $ 2,205 / year	—
Surviving spouse	$10,580 / year	$432
Surviving spouse + one dependent	$13,249 / year	$566
Each additional dependent child	Add $2,205 / year	—

Who Qualifies for Housebound Pension Benefits?
You may be eligible for Housebound allowance if:

- You have a permanent disability that has been rated as 100 percent disabling AND, because of the disabling condition(s), you are permanently and substantially confined to your home.

- You have a permanent disability that has been rated as 100 percent disabling AND another disabling condition(s) that are separately rated as 60 percent or more disabling.

If you are applying for Housebound benefits, make certain to submit sufficient medical records and physicians' evaluations. You want to ensure your application demonstrates that your disability inhibits your ability to leave the immediate premises.

Aid and Attendance (A&A) Level

Aid and Attendance is the highest rate of VA Pension for a qualifying veteran or the single surviving spouse. The Aid and Attendance medical rating can often reduce the cost of care for veterans and surviving spouses who require assisted living, in-home care and private-pay nursing homes.

A&A pension allowances can provide a considerable amount of yearly cash. Below are the VA's 2017 Maximum Annual Pension Rates (MAPR) available for Aid and Attendance. Benefits became effective December 1, 2016 and include a 0.3% Cost-of-Living Increase effective December 1, 2016.

Household Status	*A&A MAPR*	*Medical Deduction*: Expenses must exceed 5% of MAPR or:
A veteran alone	$21,531/year	$645
A veteran + one dependent	$25,525/year	$845

Household Status	A&A MAPR	Medical Deduction: Expenses must exceed 5% of MAPR or:
Each additional dependent child	Add $2,205/year	—
Surviving spouse	$13,836/year	$432
Surviving spouse + one dependent	$16,506/year	$566
Each additional dependent child	Add $2,205/year	—

Who Qualifies for Aid and Attendance Pension Benefits?

To qualify for A&A, in addition to being eligible for basic pension, the veteran or surviving spouse must also meet at least one of the following criteria:

- You require the help of another person in activities of daily living (ADL) — or —
- You have a mental or physical disability that demands regular care and assistance — or —
- Disabilities have substantially confined you to a bed — or —
- You suffer from disabling vision impairments — or —
- You suffer from mental or physical disabilities requiring nursing home care.

If you are applying for Aid and Attendance, make certain to submit solid medical evidence, including medical records and physicians' evaluations. You want to ensure your application demonstrates that your disability inhibits your ability to complete activities of daily living and that you need the assistance of a caregiver.

Under some circumstances, a family member may receive an Aid and Attendance stipend as a non-licensed home caregiver. Your advisor will help you determine whether or not that is possible.

A good source of information can be found at the local Veterans of Foreign Wars (VFW) chapter or the American Legion.[23]

An Example of Determining Financial Need
for Aid and Attendance

Suppose you meet the eligibility requirements for age or disability, and military service. Do you meet the financial requirements? The following shows one scenario for a veteran and spouse.

Example:

Daniel, a resident of Levy County, Florida, is a 76-year-old wartime veteran with a debilitating back disorder and mobility impairment. In need of Aid and Attendance, Daniel has applied for VA Pension. As a veteran with one dependent, in 2017 he is eligible for up to $25,525 in VA Pension, including A&A allowance.

Income/Net Worth: Daniel's wife Ana receives $17,000 a year from Social Security. Daniel earns about $21,000 a year from Social Security. Ana also receives a retirement pension in the amount of $2,000 per year. This is the bulk of the couple's annual income and net worth and adds up to $40,000.

Their household earns more than the annual Aid and Attendance MAPR of $25,525. However, they have not determined their expenses yet. If they have recurring unreimbursed medical expenses (UME), they may have deductions that could reduce the countable income to the point that they qualify. This will be the Income for VA Purposes (IVAP).

Medical Expenses: Their combined health care expenses include Medicare premiums of $240/month, and the cost of Daniel's physical therapy and home health services, totaling $2,500/month. These medical expenses add up to $32,880 a year.

Subtract 5 percent of MAPR for this category: $845

Adjusted Medical Expenses (after deduction):

$32,880 – $845 = $32,035/year.

IVAP: Next, the couple determines the IVAP. They deduct their (adjusted) medical expenses from their annual gross income: $40,000 – $32,035 = $7,965 IVAP.

Now they can figure their pension benefit. They subtract the IVAP from the maximum annual pension (MAPR):

$25,525 – $7,965 = $17,560/year.

Since the maximum benefit Daniel can receive is $25,525 (basic pension with Aid and Attendance allowance), Daniel and Ana are eligible to receive $17,560 a year in Aid and Attendance pension.

Even though the couple's income is over the MAPR, the unreimbursed medical expenses that the couple is currently paying for personally will put the couple's "countable income" well within range of eligibility.

How to Prove Aid and Attendance Needs

VA Pension is not an entitlement. The veteran must prove he or she deserves/has earned an award of pension. If your application is insufficient, wrong or otherwise fails to demonstrate that you meet all eligibility requirements, the VA will question your application, require further information (thus delaying any award) or, in some cases, find you to be ineligible from the start.

Proving you qualify for Aid and Attendance requires demonstrating that your situation includes one of the following situations:

- You are completely bedridden and must stay in bed to continue treatment.

- You require assistance from another person to perform activities of daily living (ADLs), which include requiring personal assistance with bathing, toileting, feeding, dressing, getting in and out of a bed or chair, walking, daily hygiene or help with managing prosthetics.

- You need daily assistance adjusting prosthetic or orthopedic devices.
- You need daily assistance to remain safe from hazards and dangers within a routine environment.
- You are currently in an assisted living facility or nursing home due to mental or physical incapacity.
- You meet the VA's criteria for blindness (your corrected visual acuity is 5/200 or less).

These circumstances can be proved with medical records, which will be sent to the VA upon applying for the benefits. Make sure your medical records are as thorough and detailed as possible, and show specifically what you can and cannot do for yourself. Keep all records of treatment, expenses, tax forms and other pertinent accounting records and documentation.

Can a Veteran Receive Both VA Pension and VA Disability Compensation at the Same Time?

No. If you are currently receiving disability compensation (service-connected) from the VA, you cannot receive both the compensation and pension (non-service connected).

You may switch from compensation to pension. In this case, as part of your pension application, you should inform the VA of your intent to change benefits. If you apply for and are awarded pension benefits, the VA will typically award whichever benefit is greater; however, it is in your best interest to fully evaluate both benefits for your situation.

How Does a Surviving Spouse/Dependent Child Qualify for Veteran's Pension?

A surviving spouse may qualify for non-service connected benefits, such as pension, if the deceased veteran fulfilled all of his or her service requirements and:

- the spouse has an income below the yearly limit, set by Congress, to be eligible for pension benefits, and
- the spouse continuously lived with the veteran from the date of marriage until the veteran's death and have not remarried (with certain exceptions).

Dependent children may be eligible for Survivors' Pension if they are

- not married, AND
- younger than 18 or between ages 18 and 23, if attending school, OR
- are permanently incapable of self-support due to a disability incurred before age 18.

How Does Pension Affect Eligibility for Supplemental Security Income (SSI)?

Similar to VA Pension, SSI is a needs-based governmental program that provides a monthly check to individuals who are blind, elderly or have a disability. For these individuals, who have never worked (and are therefore not eligible for Social Security Disability), SSI is often the only program available.

It is possible for a veteran to receive SSI and VA Pension at the same time. However, your SSI benefits will be reduced or you may be ineligible for any payments. Remember, these are different programs, with their own eligibility requirements and separate definitions of disability that must be met.

SSI benefit payments are based on a federal benefit rate. In 2017, this rate is $735/month for a single person and $1,103/month for married couples. Most states, including Florida, add money to the federal SSI payment.

It is generally accepted that the SSI payment is going to be less than the basic VA Pension amounts. However, in the case of a surviving spouse, if their VA Pension is less than the federal SSI, then they would be eligible to receive both payments, although they would only receive some of the SSI amount, not necessarily the full amount.

How Will Veterans Pension Affect Medicaid Eligibility?

Both the Medicaid program and Veterans Pension (Aid and Attendance) can assist aging or disabled veterans (and their spouses) with long-term care options for assisted living facilities and nursing home care.

The Medicaid program is completely separate and very different from the Department of Veterans Affairs. Medicaid provides medical coverage to low-income individuals and families. Costs of the Medicaid program are shared by the State of Florida and the federal government. Florida Medicaid services are administered by the Agency for Health Care Administration. Medicaid eligibility in Florida is determined either by the Department of Children and Families (DCF) or the Social Security Administration (for SSI recipients).[24]

Ineligibility for Medicaid Benefits
While Aid and Attendance is a great help for many veterans, Aid and Attendance cannot fully cover the costs of long-term care needs.

Without comprehensive planning, it can become a serious road block to some veterans who need to remain eligible for certain Medicaid programs.

You may one day need to qualify for Medicaid to cover nursing home and other long-term care expenses. Yet the wrong planning techniques can disqualify you from being allowed to receive Medicaid benefits. Situations that qualify you for VA Aid and Attendance may prohibit access to Medicaid benefits for several critical years.

How Medicaid and VA Pension can operate together and actually coordinate with each other is a complex and tricky subject. For a more in-depth look, please see Chapter 4: "The Interplay between Florida Medicaid Benefits and VA Benefits," and Chapter 5: "Legal Strategies for Obtaining Non-Service Connected Pension Benefits."

How to Apply for Non-Service Connected VA Pension Benefits

1. File Online (VONAPP).
   Go to: www.eBenefits.VA.gov/ebenefits/vonapp

2. File with paper application VA Form 21-527EZ, "Application for Pension," and mail it to the Pension Management Center (PMC) having jurisdiction over your claim. If you are unsure which Pension Management Center is correct, you may submit your application to the VA regional office closest to you. You can locate your local Regional Benefit Office using the VA Facility Locator (www.VA.gov).

3. You may fax the claim to VA's centralized fax number: 844-531-7878

4. To apply for increased pension based on Aid and

Attendance or Housebound payments, write to the PMC that serves your state and provide medical evidence, such as a doctor's report, that validates the need for an increased benefit.

5. Surviving spouses: to apply for Survivors Pension, download and complete VA Form 21-534EZ, "Application for DIC, Death Pension, and/or Accrued Benefits." Mail the completed form to the Pension Management Center (PMC) that serves your state. You may also visit your local Regional Benefit Office and turn in your application for processing. You can locate your local Regional Benefit Office using the VA Facility Locator (www.va.gov).

6. Fully Developed Claims (FDC): Fast track your claim review by submitting a "Fully Developed Claim" (explained below).

7. Appoint a VA-accredited attorney or agent to act on your behalf.

Fully Developed Claim (FDC) Program — VA Pension

The Fully Developed Claim (FDC) program has been developed to speed up the claim processing time. The FDC program is optional, and, as explained in Chapter 2, FDC is used for disability compensation claims as well as pension claims.

For a Veterans Pension claim or Survivors Pension claim to be processed as a fully developed claim, it must contain all supporting forms and evidence, including discharge papers, medical evidence and records, and complete marital information. If you are seeking benefits for Aid and Attendance, the form must include documentation of the cost of the care being provided and documentation that the care is meeting the needs described in the doctor's report.

If you file a claim for VA Pension in the FDC Program and it is determined that other records exist that VA needs in order to decide your claim, then VA will remove the claim from the FDA Program and process it in the Standard Claim Process.

If the VA finds that the any required documentation is missing, they will reassign the claim into regular processing. That way, there is no risk to the veteran or survivor claimant (other than delay) when submitting a FDC.

For more information about the Fully Developed Claim program, please see the final section of Chapter 2, "Fully Developed Claims (FDC) Program — Disability Compensation."

For assistance in completing your claim in the best light, consider contacting a VA accredited attorney. This also holds true if you are filing a Fully Developed Claim, because you don't want to mistakenly leave something out or submit the wrong information.

A qualified lawyer will have the experience necessary to successfully file and handle VA Pension claims and appeals, and can be highly beneficial in helping you obtain your rightful benefits.

Finally, other benefits are available to disabled veterans. A good attorney will help you consider all possible benefits, as this may result in receiving additional stipend for your military service, while helping to provide important support when you need it most.

Chapter 4

The Interplay Between Florida Medicaid Benefits and VA Benefits

As previously mentioned, veterans in need of long-term care may find possible financial help through either VA Pension or Medicaid benefits. Navigating Medicaid and Veterans Pension on your own is a tremendous challenge. It can cost you literally tens of thousands of dollars a year if you don't have the right information or take the wrong approach. When deciding which benefit to apply for in your unique situation, it is most beneficial to seek legal advice from an Elder Law attorney who is accredited by the Department of Veterans Affairs and specializes in Medicaid planning.

Taking the wrong path, and making the wrong choices, can bring financial harm to aging or disabled veterans and their families. With proper legal counsel and preparation, many veterans and spouses find they qualify for significant benefits they did not think were available to them.

Eligibility Requirements for
VA Pension Versus Medicaid Benefits

As a veteran or veteran's spouse in need of nursing home or assisted living care, you may qualify for benefits from Florida Medicaid as well as from the VA. The financial requirements for eligibility for VA Pension and Medicaid benefits are both based on limited income and assets.

Veterans and their spouses should examine and weigh the eligibility requirements for both VA Pension (Aid and Attendance or Housebound benefits) and Medicaid very carefully. If you are a single veteran, you cannot receive Medicaid nursing home care and VA Pension at the same time. However, you may need one or the other type of benefit at different stages of your life. (If you are an unmarried individual in a nursing home on Medicaid, you can still receive $90 per month in VA Aid and Attendance.)

On the other hand, a married veteran and spouse could simultaneously be eligible for benefits from both programs; one spouse could receive A&A Pension while the other receives Medicaid benefits.

Depending on your situation, qualifying for VA Aid and Attendance may involve planning techniques. This could entail divestment, gifting, transferring and other forms of restructuring assets to lower your income to an amount that meets the Department of Veterans Affairs' maximum income requirements. Transferring assets to meet VA Pension financial limits can be a double-edged sword, because such actions may be penalized under Medicaid rules.

Additionally, your Medicaid caseworker may require that, before your Medicaid application can be approved, you must first apply for VA benefits. Any VA Pension you receive will transfer a portion of the cost paid by Medicaid to the Veterans Administration.

Aid and Attendance Versus Medicaid: What's the Difference?

In the table below, we can see at a glance some clear differences between A&A and Medicaid for veterans and their surviving spouses.

Florida Medicaid Versus VA Aid & Assistance

Feature	Florida Medicaid	VA Pension: Aid & Attendance
Gov't. Level	State/Federal Partnership	Federal
2017 Countable Income Limits	$2,205/mo. (an individual)	$1,794/mo. (a veteran alone - MAPR)
	No Maximum Limit (well spouse)	$2,127/mo. (veteran + 1 dependent - MAPR)
2017 Countable Asset Limits	$2,000 assets (an individual)	$40,000–$50,000 (a net worth "ballpark estimate" for a veteran alone)
	Up to $120,900 (well spouse)	$80,000 (a net worth "ballpark estimate" for a veteran and non-veteran spouse)
Benefit is most appropriate for:	Nursing Home Care, Assisted Living Facility, In-Home Care	In-Home Care or Assisted Living Faciility

Note: Data cited are approximate as various conditions and exceptions will occur.

Medicaid is a health insurance program for needy individuals. To qualify for Medicaid, a claimant who is single must have a limited amount of assets (less than $2,000) and monthly income (less than $2,205, or a qualified income trust will need to be established), and be substantially unable to pay for his or her care expenses.

Medicaid will generally pay for long-term care services, including nursing home, assisted living facilities and in-home care services.

VA Aid and Attendance Pension is a needs-based cash benefit. For example, A&A will provide an annual allowance of: $21,531 to a single veteran; $25,525 to a veteran with one dependent; $13,836 to a surviving spouse, and; $16,506 to a surviving spouse with one dependent. The beneficiary must have insufficient income and assets to meet his or her care needs, according to VA rules.

When Is VA Pension the Right Way to Go, and When Is Medicaid the Better Strategy?

There is much to consider, and every circumstance is unique. While the VA Aid and Attendance benefit is a valuable aid to veterans needing long-term care, the Medicaid program can be a more suitable program for certain individuals who require long-term care in a skilled nursing facility. Yes, a veteran's Aid and Attendance allowance can certainly be used toward nursing home care, and it may be the right solution for you. However, the maximum A&A benefit is generally far less than the typical cost of assisted living and nursing home care in Florida.

For these and many other reasons, always seek qualified counsel to determine the right strategies for your circumstance. Various other planning tools may be used, as well, to provide additional funds for long-term care costs.

Pros and Cons a Veteran Should Know About Aid and Attendance Versus Medicaid

There can be various steps along the way of an elder or disabled veteran's journey. Many will require Medicaid benefits, at some point, to pay for skilled nursing home care.

For instance, a veteran may start out using the VA Aid and Attendance pension. But pension often turns out to be just a small slice of what the elder veteran will eventually need. One medical event can trigger the immediate need for permanent custodial care in a skilled nursing home. The financial toll this type of long-term care can inflict on an unprepared family is astonishing.

Receiving Pension May Disqualify a Veteran for Medicaid Benefits

VA Aid and Attendance and Medicaid may appear to be similar, in some respects, because they are both needs-based programs. But that is where the similarities end. The eligibility rules are quite different, and planning strategies for VA Pension and Medicaid are very distinct. Careful coordination between VA Pension and Medicaid planning is essential.

In fact, receiving VA Pension may prevent a veteran's eligibility for Medicaid benefits. Problems arise when a veteran, who recently transferred assets to qualify for A&A, suddenly realizes he or she needs to qualify for Medicaid to cover the soaring long-term care expenses. For example:

- If you have transferred or gifted assets or income to qualify for VA Pension, Medicaid will find you ineligible for benefits. Under Medicaid, recent asset transfers are not allowed; you are penalized with a five-year "look back" period. Medicaid will look back over the last five years of your financial activities. You would have to reapply after the five year period elapsed.

- In VA Pension planning, (as of this writing) the transfer of a claimant's assets is allowed with no look back penalty. [Note: these parameters will likely change going forward in 2017 — see Chapter 7, Veterans Benefits: What Does the Future Hold?]

Example:

Sam's father, Fred, is a resident of Putnam County, Florida and has received Aid and Attendance benefits for the past year and a half, comfortably residing in an assisted living facility. To qualify for A&A, his father transferred $400,000 in assets into Sam's name.

Sam's father is now dealing with Alzheimer's and will require skilled nursing home care. Realizing that the A&A pension allowance cannot cover the costs of the care his father now needs (about $9,000 a month), Sam applies for Medicaid benefits for his father.

Sam quickly finds out that he must wait out the remainder of Medicaid's five-year look-back penalty period (or return the assets to Fred, which will then cause Fred to be ineligible for Medicaid, because of the $2,000 Medicaid asset limit) before his father will be eligible. Sam did not know that Medicaid imposed a penalty on recent asset transfers. This severely limits Sam's father's ability to access the skilled care and living arrangement he needs. With proper A&A and Medicaid planning, Sam could have avoided this result completely.

The Solution Lies in Legal, Allowable Asset Planning Strategies

There are acceptable ways to move and preserve your assets. These strategies are the essence of Medicaid planning. By restructuring your countable assets into exempt assets, you can obtain VA Aid & Attendance benefits, maintain eligibility for Medicaid benefits, and shelter and preserve your personal legacy.

Furthermore, many veterans or surviving spouses live well into their 80s or 90s without needing any assistance, yet it is prudent to have a plan in place.

Example:

Janice, a resident of Nassau County, Florida is the 82-year-old widow of a WWII veteran. She is healthy, independent and stays on the go. Janice recently sold her and her deceased husband's home and moved into a smaller, more manageable house in the same neighborhood to remain close to her friends. If Janice becomes incapacitated, she and her attorney know she is eligible for Veterans Aid and Attendance Pension because of her late husband's service. Her attorney is well-versed in the different processes used by both the VA Pension and the Medicaid programs when determining countable income, the different asset limits and the laws governing each. Janice has taken the steps necessary to legally structure her finances so she will qualify for the appropriate benefit program when the time comes.

How Much Nursing Home Cost Does VA Pension Cover?

The monthly VA Aid and Attendance allowance is rarely enough to cover nursing home costs. As explained in Chapter 3, the VA's Maximum Annual Pension Rates (MAPR) that is available for Aid and Attendance is (approximately):

- $21,531 yearly for a single veteran
- $25,525 yearly for a married veteran
- $13,836 yearly for a surviving spouse

In 2016, the median annual rate for a semi-private room in a Florida nursing home was $89,000.[25] That leaves a tremendous gap in coverage. Medicaid can generally cover the difference in cost and the veteran's ability to pay. For many if not most situations, Medicaid is the better option.

When Medicaid Is Awarded, VA Pension May be Reduced

If Medicaid is paying for your care, you may still receive the VA Pension benefit; however, the benefit amount is reduced to about $90/month (for an unmarried recipient of A&A).

For a single veteran (or surviving spouse) with no dependent children — who is either eligible for Medicaid or is in a nursing home and on Medicaid — the VA will not pay the full pension amount. Instead, the VA pays $90 a month towards nursing home costs. In other words, once you enter a nursing home and qualify for Medicaid, any pension you had qualified for is, by law, reduced.

Rather than applying the $90 toward nursing home payments, Florida allows the entire $90 to be used for the patient's monthly personal needs allowance, if desired. The allowance pays for items not covered by Medicaid or Medicare, such as toiletries and personal hygiene items, clothing, beauty or barber shop services, books and phone service.

Under Florida Medicaid rules, the $90 VA Pension is not considered as "countable income" for Medicaid eligibility purposes.[26]

Strategies for Married Couples

Circumstances for married couples are unique. As mentioned earlier, it is possible for one spouse to receive Medicaid benefits while the other receives VA Pension. So, it is wise for a veteran household to check into the eligibility for both.

Example 1:

Bill, a resident of Suwannee County, Florida, is a Korean War veteran with a dependent non-veteran spouse, Patty. Both individuals are low income. Bill is in good health and lives in their home. His wife Patty lives in an assisted living community. She has difficulty with mobility, dressing and bathing. Most of Patty's care expenses are paid for by VA Aid and Attendance pension.

Two years pass, and Bill has a stroke. He now needs custodial care in a nursing home. While his wife's health care costs are handled through his VA Pension, Bill is still eligible to file for Florida Medicaid to cover the yearly costs of the nursing home.

Example 2:

Harry, a resident of Wakulla County, Florida, is a wartime veteran whose mind is faltering and health is declining. His wife Susan is a healthy 72-year-old non-veteran, but is getting too frail to help Harry with many of the ADLs. The family makes the tough decision to place Harry in a nursing home. With the help of her attorney, Susan applies for both VA Aid and Attendance and Medicaid, simultaneously. Harry and Susan's household income and assets are too high for Medicaid eligibility, so they must go through the Medicaid "spend down." While Susan goes about the process of spending down their assets, VA Pension will be there to provide additional money for nursing home costs in the meantime. When Harry becomes eligible for Medicaid, Medicaid benefits will then kick in to cover his nursing home costs.

While Susan is living, VA will continue to pay the Aid and Attendance benefit amount. Under Medicaid rules, the A&A portion of Pension is exempt income. Upon Mary's death, VA reduces the amount to $90/month.

Consolidate Your Plans!

To make good decisions, you must have a complete sense of all of the benefit programs and legal options available to you as a veteran or surviving spouse. Understanding how Veterans Pension works in conjunction with Medicaid benefits is a big part of an elder veteran's life care plan. Protect your Medicaid eligibility! If you do not need Medicaid now, you may need it later. Take steps to coordinate Florida Medicaid, Veterans benefits, Medicare and any private health insurance that you have. Make them work together whenever possible.

The legal planning and administrative work required to accomplish these types of planning strategies are highly complex. Only an attorney who is accredited by the VA and fully knowledgeable about Medicaid planning can help you explore the full spectrum of asset protection options available, and plan the ones that are right for you. Whether planning for VA Pension or Medicaid, legal strategies for restructuring and transferring assets are the solution.

In the following chapter, we take a look at real life examples of how you can, with proper counsel, legally restructure your assets to get the Veterans Aid & Attendance and/or Medicaid benefits you need.

Keep in mind that the qualifying processes and guidelines for VA Pension with Aid and Attendance allowance are set to change going forward into 2017. We have a special section of Chapter 7 set aside to explain what to expect with VA Pension planning.

Chapter 5

Legal Strategies for Obtaining Non-Service Connected Pension Benefits

Asset Restructuring for VA Aid and Attendance Benefits

As previously discussed, the VA Aid and Attendance program has limits. As a general rule, countable assets in excess of $80,000 would typically be too high to obtain VA Aid & Attendance for a married VA claimant. If the VA claimant (the veteran or the veteran's surviving spouse) is unmarried, then countable assets in excess of $40,000 may be too high.

Additionally, the VA uses a process called "age analysis" when determining eligibility for VA Aid and Attendance. This means that the older the VA claimant is, the lower the countable assets will need to be, in order to be eligible for A&A benefits. In determining eligibility, the VA uses a standard of whether or not the claimant has sufficient means to pay for his or her care for the rest of the claimant's life. The

VA uses actuarial tables, based on a person's age and standardized life expectancy, to determine whether or not the claimant's funds will be sufficient to pay for a person's care.

Example:

Fred, a resident of Indian River County, Florida, is a 97-year-old World War II veteran who owns $75,000 in countable assets. Fred lives in an assisted living facility, which costs $3,000 per month. Fred receives pension and Social Security totaling $2,500 per month, leaving Fred with a $500 per month shortage, in terms of paying the assisted living facility each month.

Fred applied for VA Aid & Attendance benefits, fully expecting to receive the special monthly pension, because he had heard that the asset limit for VA Aid & Attendance was $80,000. Fred was very surprised when his VA application was denied, as he only had $75,000 in countable assets. The reason the VA denied his application was because the VA used age analysis in determining his eligibility.

Based on Fred's actuarial life expectancy under the actuarial tables, the VA determined that Fred, at the age of 97, had sufficient funds to pay for his own care for the rest of his life.

What Are the Exempt Assets for VA Aid and Attendance?

The following assets are treated as exempt assets, in terms of determining a claimant's eligibility for VA Aid and Attendance: one home, one automobile, life insurance policies with no cash value, a burial plot, a funeral service or cremation contract, household items and certain types of annuities with no cash value.

What Are Countable Assets for VA Aid and Attendance?

The following types of assets are treated as countable assets, in terms of determining a VA claimant's eligibility for VA Aid and Attendance: Bank accounts, stocks, bonds, real estate, real estate other than homestead, IRAs, life insurance with cash value and annuities with cash value.

Asset Restructuring Strategies to Obtain VA Benefits

There are a number of different legal strategies that can be used to restructure or protect countable assets, so that a prospective claimant may become qualified for VA Aid and Attendance.

When implementing the strategies, it is important to keep in mind that VA asset restructuring strategies do not all work the same way that Medicaid asset restructuring strategies work. Conversely, some Medicaid asset restructuring strategies will not work as VA restructuring strategies. The reason why this may be a critical issue in any given case is that the VA claimant may someday need nursing home care, if the VA claimant's health deteriorates.

As of the publication of this book, the average cost of nursing home care in Florida is approximately $8,700 per month. The maximum VA Aid and Attendance rates are nowhere near as high as the average cost of nursing home care in Florida, so the VA claimant may someday need to apply for Florida Medicaid, if the claimant ever has to go to a nursing home.

Example:

Gertrude, a resident of Clay County, Florida, the surviving spouse of a World War II veteran who is 87 years old, was residing in an assisted living facility that cost $2,800 per month. Gertrude had previously applied for VA Aid and Attendance, and she was receiving the 2017 maximum pension amount of $1,153. Along with her Social Security in the amount of $1,470.90 per month, and the $20,000 she had saved in her checking account, Gertrude was able to pay for the assisted living bill each month.

To obtain VA benefits, Gertrude had hired an Elder Law attorney two years ago to help. The Elder Law attorney had recommended the use of an irrevocable VA Asset Protection Trust (to be discussed later in this chapter), to shelter $150,000 of Gertrude's countable assets, thereby reducing Gertrude's assets within the VA parameters.

The Elder Law attorney had advised Gertrude that this type of asset protection trust would only work to restructure her assets to obtain VA Aid and Attendance benefits. The irrevocable trust would not work as a Medicaid planning strategy, if Gertrude had to go into a nursing home and apply for nursing home Medicaid, within five years of establishing the asset protection trust. Gertrude has recently been hospitalized, after suffering a severe stroke while playing shuffle board at the assisted living facility. Her doctor is now recommending that Gertrude be placed long term in a nursing facility, in the hopes that she will someday recover from her stroke and be able to return to the assisted living facility.

Along with the $20,000 in Gertrude's checking account, and the $150,000 held in the VA irrevocable trust, Gertrude is well over the $2,000 asset limit for Florida nursing home Medicaid. Fortunately, the attorney who drafted the VA trust was experienced. He had drafted the trust in such a way that the assets held in the trust could be removed from the trust, and returned to Gertrude, within the five-year look-back period. Then the assets could be restructured, along with the $20,000 in Gertrude's checking account, so that Gertrude will now be able to obtain Florida Medicaid coverage while she is in the nursing home.

The following are strategies that can be used in Florida to restructure assets and bring the prospective VA claimant within the permissible asset guidelines, in order to obtain VA Aid & Attendance benefits:

Purchase of Homestead

The M21-1 Compensation and Pension Manual of the VA states that the home of the VA claimant does not count as an asset, when determining eligibility for VA Aid and Attendance. This means that, if the prospective VA claimant does not currently own a home, the claimant would be able to purchase a home, and that home would not count toward the VA claimant's countable assets limits.

Example:

Leo is a 92-year-old resident of Pinellas County, Florida who is also a World War II veteran. Leo has been living in an apartment by himself since his wife died seven years ago. Leo's only child, Aphrodite, has recently become concerned about some issues that Leo has been having with his memory, as well as some increasingly serious vision problems due to macular degeneration. Leo has been receiving shots from the eye doctor to slow down his macular degeneration, but Leo's vision has gotten much worse in the past six months.

Leo's primary physician is now recommending that Leo may need assisted living care within the next 12 months.

Other than a car, Leo has approximately $300,000 in bank accounts, which far exceeds the VA's asset limit for VA

Aid and Attendance. Leo and his daughter Aphrodite consult with an Elder Law attorney and learn that the purchase of a Florida homestead would be treated as an exempt asset for VA Aid and Attendance purposes.

Leo makes the decision to move out of his apartment, and purchase a $250,000 home in Tarpon Springs, Florida. Aphrodite has agreed to move in, to take care of Leo, while he is living in his new home. If Leo needs to move into an assisted living facility at some point in the future, his home will be treated as an exempt asset. Also, if Leo ever needs to go to a nursing home, the $250,000 purchase amount for his home would be exempt for Medicaid purposes.

The Purchase of an Automobile of Any Value

One automobile is also exempt, under the VA rules. Accordingly, it is permissible to purchase an automobile to restructure countable assets into exempt assets.

Example:

Ginger is an 81-year-old resident of Broward County, Florida. Ginger is a surviving spouse of an eligible veteran, Charles, who served honorably for three years during the Korean War. Charles died two years ago, and Ginger was recently admitted to an assisted living facility. Ginger owns the $200,000 condominium where she had previously lived, and she has $85,000 in a checking account. Ginger decides to purchase a $55,000 Cadillac so she can take her children around Broward County when they come to visit her in Florida. The $55,000 Cadillac is an exempt asset under VA rules, and Ginger has successfully reduced her countable assets from $85,000 to $30,000. She is now likely within the asset parameters to become eligible for the VA Aid and Attendance program.

The Use of a Personal Services Contract

A personal services contract can be used to reduce countable assets for VA planning purposes. A personal services contract is a legal agreement, structured and drafted by a Florida attorney to pay individuals who spend time caring for other individuals. Some family members are heavily involved in the care of their family members who are at home, in an assisted living facility or in a nursing home.

Under Section 61 of the Internal Revenue Code (IRC 61, 26 U.S.C. § 61), the payment to others in exchange for their caregiver services constitutes gross income. However, the payment to a caregiver would be a viable way to reduce assets to become eligible for VA Aid and Attendance benefits.

Example:

Denise, a resident of Polk County, Florida, is a 68-year-old surviving spouse of Oscar. Oscar served honorably for two years in the Vietnam War. Unfortunately, Oscar died last year from a stroke. Oscar was the primary in-home caregiver of Denise, who has multiple sclerosis.

Jennifer, Denise and Oscar's daughter, has been trying to care for her mother to keep her in the family home. Unfortunately, due to her other work and personal responsibilities, Jennifer is no longer able to spend as much time with Denise, and Denise now has to move into an assisted living facility.

Denise owns her own home and has $50,000 in her checking account. Jennifer consults with an experienced Elder Law attorney, and the attorney prepares a personal services contract to pay to Jennifer $15,000 in a lump sum, to be involved in Denise's care for the rest of Denise's life. The contract is signed by both Denise and Jennifer, and Denise issues a check to Jennifer for $15,000. Jennifer must pay income taxes on the $15,000 payment, but Denise's assets are now reduced to $35,000. Because Denise is relatively young at 67 years old, her assets are now low enough for Denise to become eligible for VA Aid and Attendance.

Repairs to the Homestead

As previously discussed, the homestead owned by the VA claimant is an exempt asset. Accordingly, repairs made to the homestead are an acceptable way to restructure countable assets into non-countable assets and reduce assets to become eligible for VA Aid and Attendance.

Example:

Arthur is an 83-year-old widower and is a resident of Manatee County, Florida. He served honorably in the Korean War for three years. Arthur owns a homestead property worth approximately $300,000, and he has $100,000 in his checking account. Arthur was recently diagnosed with prostate cancer, which the doctor advised had gone undiagnosed for a number of years. Arthur did not like going to see his doctors, and he had his last annual physical eight years ago. The cancer had developed some point during the last eight years and has now spread to Arthur's bones. Arthur, his son David and his doctor have decided that it would be best for Arthur to go into an assisted living facility now.

Arthur's monthly Social Security is only $1,100 per month, but the assisted living facility will cost $3,000 per month, leaving Arthur with a shortfall of approximately $2,000 per month.

Arthur and David consult with an Elder Law attorney and learn that repairs to the homestead are an acceptable way to reduce assets to obtain VA Aid and Attendance eligibility. Arthur has made no repairs to his home for the past 20 years. The home really needs the following repair work done: a new roof, a new HVAC system, new countertops in the kitchen, painting on both the inside and the outside of the home, a new burglar alarm, new sod and landscaping for the front and back yards, and new carpeting and tiling in all the rooms.

Upon receiving advice from the Florida Elder Law attorney, Arthur and David contacted Home Depot and discovered that they are able to find a contractor, as well as purchase all the needed repair items, through Home Depot and the contractor. Over a three-month period, the contractor purchases all the supplies and makes all requested repairs to Arthur's home. The grand total for repairs and contractor's services was $58,000. The $58,000 in total home repair expenses was a permissible way to restructure the money in Arthur's checking account, and now Arthur only has $42,000 in countable assets.

The Purchase of Other Exempt Assets

The purchase of exempt assets is a way to permissibly restructure countable assets, and obtain VA benefits.

Example:

In reference to the preceding example with Arthur and David, after spending $58,000 on repairs to Arthur's homestead, Arthur's Elder Law attorney recommends that Arthur's countable assets be reduced even further, before the VA application is submitted.

Arthur and David decide to purchase the following personal and household items for Arthur: a motorized wheelchair, hearing aids, a new refrigerator and stove for the kitchen, clothes for Arthur, a laptop computer for Arthur, a television and a new cell phone for Arthur.

The grand total for these additional personal and household items is $12,000, thereby reducing Arthur's countable assets to approximately $30,000. With the purchase of these additional items, Arthur has now sufficiently reduced his countable assets, so that Arthur will now be eligible for the VA Aid and Attendance program, when he moves into an assisted living facility.

The Payment of Debt and Expenses

The payment of debt and expenses is also a permissible way to reduce countable assets, and obtain VA benefits.

Example:

Martha is an 88-year-old resident of Citrus County, Florida and a surviving spouse of Earl, a decorated veteran of World War II who fought the Germans in France. Since Earl died, Martha has been developing increasingly severe problems. Martha and her son Max, along with her doctor's recommendation, have decided that Martha should go into an assisted living facility within the next six months.

Martha owns a home worth approximately $150,000, a 1992 Toyota Camry, and she has $50,000 in her checking account. Martha and Max consult with a Florida Elder Law attorney and learn that the payment of debts and expenses is a permissible way to reduce countable assets, to obtain VA Aid and Attendance benefits. The Elder Law attorney recommends that Martha reduce countable assets to less than $25,000. Martha currently owes $28,000 on a second mortgage on her home, and she owes $3,000 to American Express. Martha and Max decide to pay off the second mortgage and the credit card debt with the funds in Martha's checking account.

By paying off the $31,000 in debt, Martha reduces the balance in her checking account to approximately $19,000. She has now sufficiently reduced her assets to become eligible for VA Aid and Attendance benefits when she moves into the assisted living facility.

The Purchase of a Specialty Structured Annuity

Under the VA rules, certain types of annuities are exempt, for VA purposes. This works by transforming countable assets into an income stream with the purchase of the annuity. These types of annuities have no cash value, and the annuity pays an income stream to the annuitant for a term of years. Caution must be used when purchasing these types of annuities for the following three reasons:

1. This type of annuity contract is irrevocable.

2. By converting the asset into an income stream, you are reducing the countable asset value to zero, but you are also creating more income. As a general rule, the VA claimant would not want to increase his/her income, because this will possibly reduce the amount of VA Pension that the VA claimant will receive.

3. If the VA claimant needs to apply for Florida Medicaid benefits, this type of annuity can be problematic in applying for Florida Medicaid benefits.

Example:

Genevieve is an 80-year-old resident of Hernando County, Florida and is a surviving spouse of Joseph, who served honorably for two years during the Korean War. Genevieve has been diagnosed with Alzheimer's disease and will soon need care in an assisted living facility with a memory care unit.

Genevieve's daughter and power of attorney, Helene, consults with an Elder Law attorney and learns that certain types of annuities can be used to restructure assets to obtain Veterans Benefits. Genevieve owns a mobile home worth $50,000, a 1989 Honda Civic and has $50,000 in her checking account.

Helene decides that she likes the annuity option to reduce the assets. The attorney refers Helene to an annuity salesman who specializes in VA qualifying annuities to obtain VA benefits. Helene, using her power of attorney, purchases a $25,000 VA qualifying annuity in her mother's name. The annuity pays Genevieve $300 per month, but the annuity has no cash value. Helene has successfully reduced Genevieve's assets so that Genevieve will now be eligible for VA Aid and Attendance benefits.

Adding Names of Other Individuals to the Countable Assets of the VA Claimant and/or Spouse of the VA Claimant

Another way to successfully reduce assets to obtain VA Pension is to add the name of other individuals to the financial account of the VA claimant and/or the VA claimant's spouse.

Example:

Jeffrey is a 92-year-old widower, and a resident of Santa Rosa County, Florida, who honorably served in the Pacific Theater during World War II. Jeffrey owns a condo worth $85,000 in an over-55 mobile home park, and he has $50,000 in his checking account. Jeffrey has one daughter, Samantha, who is also Jeffrey's power of attorney.

Jeffrey has recently been bothered by severe arthritis, hearing problems and glaucoma, which have been causing increasingly serious problems for Jeffrey. After consulting with Jeffrey's primary physician, Jeffrey, Samantha and Jeffrey's physician all decide that Jeffrey should go to an assisted living facility within the next few months.

Jeffrey's monthly Social Security is approximately $1,500 per month, but the assisted living facility that Jeffrey likes costs $4,000 per month. Jeffrey and Samantha consult with an Elder Law attorney. They learn that, by adding Samantha's name to Jeffrey's checking account, the VA will treat Samantha as a 50 percent owner of Jeffrey's bank account — thereby reducing Jeffrey's countable assets to $25,000 (which is one-half of the $50,000 currently in Jeffrey's checking account). Accordingly, by adding Samantha's name to Jeffrey's checking account, Jeffrey has sufficiently reduced his countable assets (to $25,000), and Jeffrey is now within the asset guidelines for VA Aid and Attendance benefits.

Gifting/The Use of an Irrevocable Asset Protection VA Trust

Under current law, gifting is a permissible way to reduce countable assets to obtain VA benefits. Similarly, assets can be transferred into an irrevocable asset protection trust to reduce countable assets.

As previously mentioned in Chapter 3 (and explained further in Chapter 7), the VA is in the process of implementing a new three-year look-back rule to do away with this type of gift planning strategy. Additionally, caution must also be used when implementing this type of strategy for the following reasons:

- Once the assets have been transferred from the VA claimant's name (or the VA claimant's spouse's name), the VA claimant is relying on the person receiving the assets to safeguard those assets. Once the assets are transferred into another person's name, the assets may then be subject to the creditor claims of that individual (for example, in a lawsuit, in a bankruptcy or a divorce). If the funds are transferred into an irresponsible person's name (or a person who has a problem, such as a substance abuse or gambling problem), the assets may then be spent quickly by the person who receives those gifted assets.

- The Florida Medicaid program has a five-year look back on such transfers. These types of transfers are disqualifying for Florida Medicaid, if the person later needs Florida Medicaid.

Accordingly, an irrevocable asset protection trust may be preferable to gifting the assets to an individual, depending on the facts and circumstances of the case. The VA Asset Protection Trust has the following advantages:

- The assets held in the VA Asset Protection Trust are

generally not subject to the creditor claims of the intended beneficiaries of the money. For example, issues like civil lawsuits, bankruptcy and divorce could all potentially subject the money held outside of the trust to the legal claims of the intended beneficiaries.

• The assets held in the VA Asset Protection Trust will be managed and held responsibly by the trustee of the trust. For example, some of the intended beneficiaries may have personal issues previously mentioned such as substance abuse, gambling problems or mental health issues. Sometimes when individuals with these types of personal problems receive money they may not responsibly manage money that has been given to them.

• The trustee has the power to return the funds held in the trust to the VA claimant, if the VA claimant has to apply for Medicaid, within five years of the funding of the VA Asset Protection Trust. The VA trust will be drafted in such a way that the funds can be easily returned to the VA claimant, if the VA claimant has to go into a Florida nursing home, and needs to apply for Florida Medicaid within five years of the funding of the trust.

Example 1:

Theodore, a widower, is a 92-year-old resident of Okeechobee County, Florida. Theodore is a World War II combat veteran, and he meets the military service criteria to be qualified for VA Aid and Attendance. Theodore owns a Florida homestead worth approximately $300,000, one automobile, and he has approximately $500,000 in a bank account. Theodore has two children, Cynthia and Cathleen, and Theodore's estate plan states that Cynthia and Cathleen will receive 100 percent of Theodore's estate and equal shares when he passes away. Theodore also receives $1,000 per month in Social Security benefits.

Theodore's physician is now recommending that Theodore move into an assisted living facility, due to mobility problems, vision problems, hearing problems and other health problems. The assisted living facility will charge approximately $3,500 per month, which Theodore's monthly Social Security will not cover.

Theodore, Cynthia and Cathleen consult with a Florida Elder Law attorney about the VA Aid and Attendance program. The attorney advises that Theodore's countable assets should be reduced to less than $25,000 for Theodore to qualify for Aid and Attendance. The Elder Law attorney reviews all the various VA planning options that are available to Theodore, and Theodore and his children decide to establish an irrevocable VA Asset Protection Trust to shelter Theodore's excess assets.

The Elder Law attorney drafts the trust, and $475,000 in cash is transferred from Theodore's bank account into the VA Asset Protection Trust. Cynthia and Cathleen are named as equal beneficiaries of the trust when Theodore dies. The trust will be managed by an independent third party trustee. After the VA application is submitted, the VA application is approved, and Theodore begins to receive the maximum VA Pension rate of $1,788 per month from the VA, to help him pay for the cost of assisted living facility.

Example 2:

With reference to the preceding example, assume that Theodore must move into a skilled nursing facility three years after the irrevocable trust is funded with the $475,000. The nursing facility costs approximately $9,000 per month. Since Theodore has moved into the nursing facility before the five-year Medicaid look-back period had ended, the trustee of the irrevocable VA Asset Protection Trust will now return the $475,000 to Theodore to cure the penalty period created by the $475,000 transfer to the irrevocable asset protection trust. The Elder Law attorney can now implement appropriate Medicaid planning strategies to protect and restructure the $475,000 in assets that have been returned to Theodore to obtain Florida nursing home Medicaid.

When Theodore obtains Florida Medicaid, the entire cost of Theodore's nursing home care, in excess of his monthly income, will be paid for by the Florida Medicaid program. Once Florida Medicaid benefits are granted to Theodore, Theodore (or his representative) must file VA Form 21-0779, to notify the VA that Florida Medicaid is now covering most of Theodore's nursing home expenses (in excess of his monthly income). As a result, since Theodore no longer has any unreimbursed medical expenses in excess of his monthly income (because the Florida Medicaid program is now paying these expenses), the VA will now reduce Theodore's monthly VA Pension from the maximum monthly amount to only $90 per month. This is because the VA Aid and Attendance pension is based entirely on Theodore's monthly unreimbursed medical expenses — which he no longer has, because Florida Medicaid is now paying for all of Theodore's monthly medical expenses, in excess of his monthly income.

Purchase of a Funeral Service Contract
or a Cremation Contract

The VA rules treat a funeral service contract or a cremation service contract as an exempt asset for VA purposes. Accordingly, it is permissible to purchase this type of asset to reduce assets to obtain VA Aid and Attendance pension benefits.

Example:

Mary is a resident of Sarasota County and is 89 years old. Mary is the widow of World War II veteran, Joseph. Joseph served honorably during World War II and met all the service criteria for Mary to be qualified as a surviving spouse of a veteran. Joseph passed away five years ago, and Mary did not remarry after Joseph's death. Mary now needs assisted living care, and her monthly Social Security is $900 per month. The assisted living facility that Mary is moving into costs $2,100 per month, leaving Mary approximately $1,200 a month extra that she needs to pay, in excess of her monthly Social Security. Mary has $30,000 in her checking account.

Mary and her daughter Barbara consult with an Elder Law attorney and learn that a funeral and/or cremation contract is exempt for VA Pension purposes. Mary decides to purchase $7,000 funeral service contract. When Mary applies for VA benefits, she is approved for the maximum VA Pension rate of $1,153 for a surviving spouse, because she now has limited assets, and her Social Security each month is not sufficient to pay for the assisted living facility. The excess cost of the assisted living facility exceeds the maximum VA Pension rate ($2,100 per month – $900 = $1,200, which is more than the maximum VA Pension rate of $1,153).

Chapter 6

Other Important Considerations in VA Benefits

What Is the VA Office of General Counsel (OGC)?

In the business world, "General Counsel" is the chief legal officer, the senior attorney of a company's in-house legal department. Their purpose is to make certain that the company is operating legally at all times, upholding corporate integrity and fair practices.

Likewise, Offices of General Counsel exist throughout government departments, including the VA. They serve to ensure that the federal agencies are operating within the law, efficiently and ethically.

The VA Office of General Counsel is tasked with identifying and addressing the legal needs of the U.S. Department of Veterans Affairs.

The Office of General Counsel Serves as the VA's Chief Legal Officer. The OCG provides legal advice and services to the Secretary of Veterans Affairs — the appointed head of the VA — and to senior department staff and officials, as well as to all organizational components of the department. OCG's services cover all laws, regulations, Executive Orders and judicial precedents pertaining to the VA.[27]

VA General Counsel issues written legal opinions that have authoritative, decisive effect in court, and are used as a source of future decision making in adjudications and appeals involving Veterans Benefits.

Furthermore, OCG works to oversee that all members within VA have a veteran focus and an understanding and dedication to the business priorities of VA clients.

What Does the VA Office of General Counsel Do?

OCG's lawyers serve as partners to the Department of Veterans Affairs. They offer legal advice and expertise, including legal and litigation services, as well as support for legislative and regulatory activities.

Services are distributed among professional group staffs, each headed by Chief Counsels. Chief Counsels head up eight Law Groups, three National Practice Groups, ten Offices of Chief Counsel in the Districts, the Ethics Specialty Team, and the Office of Accountability Review.

Operations Focus on Benefitting Veterans

OCG operations include:[28]

- *Collections* — Recovers funds owed to the VA, which are returned to VA Medical Centers for use in caring for veterans.

- *Office of Accountability Review* — Ensures timely and thorough investigation of complaints regarding VA senior managers to promote better service to veterans.

- *US Court of Appeals for Veterans Claims* (CAVC) — Ensures legally sound claims appeals process for veterans; defends the Secretary's adjudication of veterans' claims for compensation and other benefits; provide adequate resourcing to ensure claims are not backlogged at the appellate stage.

- *Contracts, Construction and Leases* — Partners with VA offices to secure legally compliant contracts that strike the best bargain for veterans and ensures timely procurement of facilities for use by veterans.

- *Office of Legislative Counsel* — Develops and coordinates the department's response to, and provides legal advice regarding, Congressional oversight requests and hearings; increases transparency and improves trust in the VA, which benefits veterans.

- *Accreditation of Veterans Representatives* — Ensures timely review, approval and oversight of the accreditation process, which improves veterans' access to qualified representatives.

- *Legally Compliant VA Programs* — Ensures legally compliant implementation of new laws and that VA programs carry out the intended purpose of serving veterans; protects the VA from litigation outcomes that are costly or inhibit efficient provision of service to veterans.

- *Information Law* — Ensures timely and complete analysis and legally appropriate release of information, whether to Congress, veterans, courts or the public; improves trust in VA, which benefits veterans.

- *Represents the VA* at Equal Employment Opportunity Commission (EEOC), Merit Systems Protection Board (MSPB) Arbitrations — Defending the agency promotes just results and protects agency resources; protects whistle blowers; ensures disciplinary actions are sound and defends them on appeal, to promote better service to veterans.

- *Tort Claims* — Strives to complete review of tort claims within 180 days, since veterans, or their families, file a majority of claims against VA.

VA Accredited Attorneys and Agents

Veterans disability compensation and veterans pension claims can be quite complicated. Often, the opportunity for a veteran to meet with an experienced attorney to review the challenges they face can be the key to obtaining all the benefits they are due, as swiftly as possible.

While any veteran can prepare and file his or her own claim for benefits with the VA, not just anyone can assist a veteran with a claim for VA benefits. By law, the assisting person must have formally applied for, trained for and received authority from the VA to represent a veteran seeking benefits. This applies even for *pro bono* work. This authority from the federal government is known as "accreditation."

VA accreditation is for the sole and limited purpose of preparing, presenting and prosecuting claims before VA, and is necessary to ensure that claimants for VA benefits have responsible, qualified representation.

Who Can Be Accredited by the VA to Assist a Veteran in a Claim?

Only certain approved veterans' organizations and private individuals can legally represent a veteran, service member, dependent or survivor before the Department of Veterans Affairs.

Recognized organizations and individuals include:

- VA accredited attorneys
- VA accredited claims agents
- Congressionally chartered Veterans Service Organizations (VSOs) — Some VSOs are "chartered," meaning they are federally approved by the VA Secretary to prepare, present and prosecute claims under laws administered by the VA.

To receive this accreditation, a lawyer, agent or VSO representative must apply to be admitted to practice before the VA, undergo a background investigation, complete specific legal education courses about the VA claims process and complete an examination.

The Office of General Counsel is responsible for accrediting attorneys and agents. One of the eight Law Groups within the OCG is the Benefits Law Group. This group is charged with overseeing VA accreditation and representation.

A searchable list of accredited attorneys, representatives and agents is available at the following two website addresses:

1. VA OCG: http://www.va.gov/ogc/apps/accreditation/
2. eBenefits: https://www.ebenefits.va.gov/ebenefits/vso-search

When Does a Veteran Need a VA Lawyer's Help?

Our discussion in Chapter 3 was about pensions and net worth: pension is a needs-based benefit, based on a veteran's annual income and net worth/assets.

Veterans with average or significant assets and income may need to pay for nursing home care or assisted living — without becoming impoverished in the process. They need help qualifying and applying for VA Pension (Aid and Attendance) or engaging in Medicaid planning. In these cases, it is important to talk with a VA-accredited attorney. It helps greatly when this person is also an experienced Elder Law attorney. You will have an experienced lawyer to guide you through all aspects of Veterans Benefits, and your attorney will be able to advise and help you with Medicaid planning and many other estate and financial planning strategies.

With the right planning, you may qualify for Aid and Attendance benefits under VA guidelines, or Medicaid benefits under Medicaid rules. Many veterans find they qualify for VA benefits they did not realize were available to them. Yet, if not done with the assistance of an attorney who has knowledge and insights into all facets of Medicaid and Veterans Benefits planning, the results can be disastrous:

- You may make the wrong choice between Medicaid and VA Aid and Attendance benefits.
- If you transfer assets as a way to qualify for Medicaid, you could lose those assets, if the right legal actions are not taken to protect them.

- Certain transfers of assets could cause ineligibility for Medicaid in ensuing years.

- Certain transfers of assets could cause ineligibility for Aid and Attendance in ensuing years.

- An application for VA benefits or Medicaid could be denied or delayed because of a mistake.

- You may miss opportunities to qualify for VA benefits you did not know you could apply for.

What Fees Will VA Accredited Attorneys, Agents and VSOs Charge?

No one may charge a fee for the filing of a VA form, prior to the filing of a Notice of Disagreement (NOD). Accordingly, VSOs assist veterans free of charge, but they may request reimbursement for extreme or uncommon expenses. VA accredited attorneys may charge a reasonable fee for their asset restructuring services.

VA reviews all fee agreements between the attorney or agent and the veteran. A copy of every fee agreement between a VA claimant and an accredited attorney or agent must be filed with the Office of the General Counsel within 30 days of its execution.

A VA accredited attorney generally takes service connected VA cases on a contingency basis, which means they only get paid on the contingency that the veteran wins on appeal. If a veteran is awarded back pay, the attorney receives a percentage of that award as their fee. If the veteran or other claimant loses the appeal, the lawyer does not get paid.

Can an Accredited Attorney or Agent Charge a Fee for Preparing an Aid and Attendance Application?

No. An accredited attorney or claims agent cannot charge for any assistance in regards to filing an original claim for VA benefits. The VA attorney or agent may only charge a fee for filing VA forms *after* the VA issues a decision on a claim and after a Notice of Disagreement has been filed. The veteran who wishes to contest the decision will file a Notice of Disagreement on the case. After the filing of the NOD, the veteran is allowed to hire an attorney or agent. At that point, the attorney or agent files a power of attorney and a fee agreement with the VA. The attorney or agent may then charge a fee for services provided.[29]

A lawyer, representative or agent may help a veteran or a claimant at no cost to file the initial VA application for benefits.

Can an Accredited Attorney or Agent Charge a Fee for Assisting with a Continuation of an Original Aid and Attendance Application?

Again the answer is no, fees cannot be charged.

Example:

Patrick was recently approved for Aid and Attendance. He was born prior to 1936 and was just advised by the VA that he may qualify for an additional year of benefits prior to his award date, if he qualifies medically and financially. To be considered, Patrick asks his attorney to help him gather and provide the following paperwork:

- A statement in support of claim requesting the earlier date of entitlement with retroactive benefits from that date (as per 38 CFR 3.400, Effective Dates).
- An Improved Pension Eligibility Verification Report (EVR).
- A Medical Expense Report Form 21P-8416 from the above requested date of entitlement to the date of Patrick's initial award date, listing all unreimbursed medical expenses (UME), such as care, prescriptions, OTC drugs up to $500 without a prescription, glasses, hearing aids, dental expenses, mileage to/ from doctors, etc.
- A letter from the doctor on letterhead stating that Patrick was either blind, or almost blind (visual acuity of 5/200 or

worse), or in need of a protective environment, or living in skilled nursing home, or in need of at least two ADLs for the entire time that the he is applying for.

- Confirmation from Patrick's care provider of assistance and care given during that period of time.

The attorney or agent is not able to charge for any of this, because it is not an adverse decision to be appealed. It is a continuation of Patrick's original A&A claim, which was approved.

What Are the Eligible Periods of Wartime Regarding VA Pension?

Eligibility for VA disability pension partly relies on the veteran having served during a period of wartime. Below are the wartime periods currently designated and considered by Congress:[30]

- Mexican Border Period   (May 9, 1916–April 5, 1917 for veterans who served in Mexico, on its borders or adjacent waters)
- World War I (April 6, 1917–November 11, 1918)
- WW II (December 7, 1941–December 31, 1946)
- Korean Conflict (June 27, 1950–January 31, 1955)
- Vietnam Era (February 28, 1961–May 7, 1975, if service was in the Republic of Vietnam)
- Vietnam Era (August 5, 1964–May 7, 1975, if service was *not* in the Republic of Vietnam)
- Persian Gulf War (August 2, 1990–Continuing, until future date is set by law or by Presidential Proclamation)

2017 Cost-of-Living Adjustment (COLA) for VA Benefits

The Social Security Administration (SSA) often applies annual Cost-of-Living Adjustment (COLA) increases to Social Security Disability Insurance (SSDI) benefits. Veterans benefits generally mirror the Social Security COLA increases.

For 2017, the increase for SSA and VA benefits will be 0.3% — a minor, if not invisible, increase. This will be the first COLA increase since 2015.

Additionally, on July 22, 2016 the Veterans' Compensation COLA Act of 2016 was signed into law. The new law orders the Department of Veterans Affairs to increase, as of December 1, 2016, the rates of veterans' disability compensation, additional compensation for dependents, the clothing allowance for certain disabled veterans, and Dependency and Indemnity Compensation (DIC) for surviving spouses and children.[31]

This bill suggests progress; it removes the need to rely on Congress to pass an increase every year. Unlike Social Security Disability benefits, which increase automatically for COLA on a yearly basis, Veterans Benefits require lawmakers to vote on the COLA adjustment each year.

Generally, the dollar amounts would be increased by the same percentage as the Social Security Disability benefits are increased, effective December 1, 2016.

Chapter 7

Veterans Benefits:
What Does the Future Hold?

Be Aware! The VA Has Proposed a New
Three-Year "Look Back" on Asset Transfers

Chapter 3 discussed how Aid and Attendance pension can help wartime veterans and surviving spouses who need assisted care in their home, a skilled nursing home or in an assisted living facility. In 2017, A&A benefits can pay up to $2,127/month for a couple, up to $1,794/month for a single veteran, and up to $1,153/month for a single surviving spouse.

To qualify for A&A, a veteran or spouse must meet income and asset requirements, and demonstrate care needs. While A&A benefits may be limited when compared to the costs of long-term care, they provide invaluable aid to the veterans who need them.

The Department of Veterans Affairs is proposing a new rule that dramatically changes and limits the benefit program. The new rule is known as Proposed Rule AO73 — Net Worth, Asset Transfers and Income Exclusions for Needs-Based Benefits.

Proposed Rule AO73 will make it tougher on veterans and spouses to qualify for Aid and Attendance benefits. There is going to be a prohibition against giving assets away to qualify for A&A benefits.

By changing basic VA regulations that control veterans' rights to Aid and Attendance and other needs-based benefit programs, the proposed rule will essentially shut off Aid and Attendance pension to many wartime veterans.

The amended regulations will:

- set forth new restrictions and conditions, involving how a veteran's net worth is evaluated, and limit how pre-application asset transfers for pension purposes can be handled;

- identify medical expenses that may be deducted from countable income for VA's needs-based benefit programs.

What Is the Reason for Proposed Rule AO73?

The proposed changes are in response to recommendations, made by the Government Accountability Office (GAO), to maintain the integrity of VA's needs-based programs. GAO was tasked with investigating how the design and management of the VA's pension program ensures that only veterans with financial need receive pension benefits. The proposed rule may also be a reflection of our rapidly growing federal deficit, as an effort to reduce government expenditures on federal entitlement programs.

As a result of their investigation, GAO recommended that Congress consider establishing a look-back and penalty period for pension claimants who transfer assets prior to applying. This is similar to the Medicaid look-back period on asset transfers.

The VA intends to clear up and address issues essential to the consistent determination of VA Pension benefits and Dependency and Indemnity Compensation (DIC) claims.

VA summarizes its objectives for the proposed three-year look-back and ten-year penalty periods in the rule's Executive Summary:

In some cases, claimants who transfer assets before applying for pension do so to create the appearance of economic need where it does not exist. By establishing a look-back and penalty period for pre-application transfers of assets, VA hopes to preserve the integrity of the pension program by ensuring that VA only pays the benefit to those with genuine need. The revised rules would also reduce opportunities for financial advisors to advise pension applicants to restructure assets that, in many cases, render the claimant ineligible for other needs-based benefits.[32]

Key Points of VA Proposed Rule AO73

The VA proposes to:[33]

1. Establish a new 36-month look-back period with a 10-year penalty period for claimants who transfer assets prior to applying for A&A.

2. Enforce a presumption that asset transfers made by the veteran during the 36-month look-back period were made to establish pension entitlement.

3. Set new, clarified net worth limits for pension entitlement. The amount of a claimant's net worth would be determined by adding the claimant's annual income to his or her assets.

4. Define and clarify how the VA calculates assets.

5. Define and clarify what the VA considers to be a deductible unreimbursed medical expense for all needs-based benefits. This may include:

    a. new definitions for many terms, such as defining activities of daily living (ADLs), and instrumental activities of daily living (IADLs)

    b. defining that custodial care means regular

assistance with two or more activities of ADLs, or assistance because a person with a mental disorder is unsafe if left alone due to the mental disorder

c. payments, such as to independent living facilities, may not be considered recurring medical expenses, as well as payments for assistance with IADLs (Exceptions would be made for disabled individuals who require health care services or custodial care.)

d. putting a limit on the hourly payment rate that the VA deducts for in-home caregivers

VA has never before imposed a penalty for transferring assets prior to applying for pension benefits. Once passed into law, the new rule will examine all transfers of assets within three years of an application for Aid and Attendance. Asset transfers that were made during the three-year look-back period could result in considerable delay (up to 10 years). To avoid the penalty, applicants will have to present clear and convincing evidence that the transfer was not made to qualify for Aid and Attendance benefits.

Unfortunately, the proposed rule will push many wartime veterans in need of care away from A&A and toward Medicaid benefits. Some war era veterans who wish to have in-home care or assisted living facility aid may lose their eligibility for A&A benefits. This may also foretell a more costly approach for state and federal Medicaid spending when compared to current VA Pension with Aid and Attendance spending.

At the time of this writing, Proposed Rule AO73 is expected to be signed into law during 2017.

It Is Now Even More Critical to Work with a Qualified Attorney

Some veterans and their spouses who truly need VA Pension with Aid & Attendance will be left without this important lifeline. While

Medicaid and A&A benefits may be available for many veterans, just as many more deserving wartime veterans, who previously were eligible, might not qualify.

The best thing to do is to be proactive. Don't wait until there is a medical need. Consider planning now for the possibility of needing care in the future.

The proposed changes to A&A benefits make it more important than ever to seek the counsel of a local VA accredited attorney. While veterans' attorneys may lose a planning opportunity for certain veterans, they serve an ever-critical role in providing veterans with the help and up-front planning they will need to qualify for VA Pension and important public benefits, such as Medicaid.

Our firm is able to provide our clients with care plans and legal advice that, instead of financially exhausting them, supports Florida veterans and their families in ways they did not know existed for them.

Just as important, our firm educates and protects clients from unscrupulous individuals who prey on veterans in need of financial aid. Many individuals and businesses hold themselves out to be veterans aid organizations, yet are nothing more than marketers selling unsuitable annuities, incompatible trust kits, mortgage schemes and more. These products can cause devastating tax problems, loss of assets and conflicts with other public benefit programs, such as Florida Medicaid.

The Federal Deficit and the Future of Veterans Benefits

Ultimately, the proposed three-year look-back provision is likely one of the government's efforts to try to reduce expenditures. Like all government expenses, it ties into the United States' exploding national deficit — spending more than it collects in taxes.

The government has issued debt for decades. The national debt is now approaching $20 trillion. As of spring 2017, the official debt of the United States government is $19.9 trillion.[34]

The Federal Reserve, as the Central Bank of the United States, is in charge of printing money, borrowing money by issuing bonds, and setting interest rates for those bonds. Over the past 50 years, the government has wildly spent and borrowed more than it has collected in revenue. That is called deficit. So, it must borrow and print even more money.

Our tax revenues are just barely sufficient to pay the interest on the national debt, let alone pay off the principal. Meanwhile, the government turns around and issues more debt to pay off old debt. And the total debt ceiling continues to rise.

This is not new information. We all know something is wrong with our Federal Reserve System (similar to some sort of legalized Ponzi scheme), but we apparently have no idea how, or the gumption to, tackle and fix it. Alas, it seems many Americans, from taxpayers to the leaders that run our country, have had their heads in the sand for decades about this deficit. We simply cannot kick this can down the road any farther.

For this very reason, our Founding Fathers had many concerns and protections against the federal government's right to borrow money. Hopefully, it will not take some sort of financial calamity before people wake up to the fact that we really do have a very serious issue. There is really no way to predict what the future holds.

How Do Veterans Benefits Contribute to the Current National Debt?

Federal expenses for Veterans Benefits have been around since the Revolutionary War. As long as we have a country to protect and defend, this will be the case.

Debt is the net accumulation of budget deficits. An overview of our government's spending distribution helps us see the top expenses, as they compose a large part of our national debt.

As of 2015, they are, in order:[35]

- *Social Programs* (63%): Health care programs (Medicare and Medicaid), Social Security program, education, housing and recreation
- *National Defense* (19%): Military spending and veterans' benefits
- *General Government and Debt Service* (13%): Executive and legislative branches, tax collection, financial management and interest payments
- *Economic Affairs and Infrastructure* (4%): Transportation, general economic and labor affairs, infrastructure projects, such as hew highways, agriculture, natural resources, energy and space
- *Public Order and Safety* (1%): Police, fire, law courts, prisons and immigration enforcement

In January 2016, the Congressional Budget Office (CBO) released its cumulative outlook of the federal budget and growing deficit for a 10-year span from 2016–2025.

According to the CBO, the most significant adjustments to expected government expenditures involve Medicaid and Veterans Benefits. CBO raised its projections of federal outlays for Medicaid to reflect higher-than-expected spending and enrollment for newly eligible beneficiaries under the Affordable Care Act. CBO also projected that expected spending for veterans disability compensation will increase substantially.[36]

How Much Does the Government Spend on Veterans Benefits?

The President's 2017 Department of Veterans Affairs' budget includes $182.3 billion. Funding will continue to support the largest transformation and upgrade in VA history; expansion and access to timely, high-quality health care and benefits; and continue efforts to end homelessness among veterans. The budget includes $78.7 billion in discretionary resources and $103.6 billion in mandatory funding.[37]

The VA is a mammoth operation. The government struggles to pay to keep their promises to the U.S. military men and women who have honorably served their country. The government's decisions regarding VA funding impacts everyone from the senior wartime veteran, to the disabled solder, to each new recruit, to the taxpayer who helps fund them all.

2017: Do Opportunities Lie Ahead?

As Admiral Mike Mullen, former Chairman of the Joint Chiefs of Staff, stated in 2011, "The single, biggest threat to our national security is our debt, so I also believe we have every responsibility to help eliminate that threat."[38]

As one presidential administration leaves office and a new administration takes over, there is hope that the road back to fiscal responsibility begins. We can also hope the new Veterans Benefits platform and 10-point plan will continue past efforts and greatly improve how veterans receive care. We have an idea how pension benefits will be impacted, but veteran and lawyer alike must wait and see the VA's final rule, when it is published.

The need for veterans to engage in long-term care planning opportunities has not changed and will only increase as changes to pension law are made. Again, it is with great respect and honor for their service and sacrifice to our country that I represent our local veterans. I cannot overstate how important it is for veterans and their beneficiaries to plan now and get the full benefits they are entitled to, rather than wait until there is urgency and medical need.

Chapter 8

Veterans Benefits Planning and the Unlicensed Practice of Law

In the past ten years, the State of Florida has seen a proliferation of non-attorney "Medicaid planners," who have been advising the public on how to obtain Medicaid benefits. Due to the proliferation of unlicensed and unregulated Medicaid planners, and to protect the public, the Florida Supreme Court approved a Medicaid Planning Advisory Opinion on January 15, 2015. The advisory opinion became final on April 10, 2015. (Advisory Opinion No. SC14-211.)[39]

In recent years, the State of Florida has also seen an increase in non-attorneys who hold themselves out as "planners" or "specialists" in the area of Veterans Benefits planning. As discussed in previous chapters in this book, in order to advise VA claimants on the processing of VA claims, both attorneys and non-attorneys must be accredited by the VA to assist VA claimants. Additionally, the State of Florida has different rules that outline the parameters of the unlicensed practice of law. Furthermore, the unlicensed practice of law is a third-degree felony, under Florida Statute 454.23.[40]

Although the Florida Supreme Court addresses only non-attorney Medicaid planners, the Advisory Opinion is based on long-standing case law and Florida legal principles, which prohibit the practice of law by non-attorneys. The Advisory Opinion addresses a number of topics, but there are a number of issues addressed in the Advisory Opinion that would apply to both non-attorney Medicaid planners and non-attorney VA planners. These activities include the following three, if performed by a non-attorney:

1. The preparation of Florida trust documents

2. The preparation of personal services contracts

3. Counseling members of the public as to the federal and state laws to obtain public benefits

Additionally, the State of Florida has seen a proliferation of non-attorney Medicaid planners "working with" Florida-licensed attorneys. This is a common practice throughout Florida and is a pattern that is also seen with non-attorney VA planners, who typically "work with" or are "affiliated with" Florida-licensed attorneys. Under the Florida Supreme Court Advisory Opinion, any attorney involved in such an arrangement with a non-attorney planner must have an independent attorney-client relationship with the client.

If you wish to report a non-attorney who is engaging in the unlicensed practice of law in Florida, you may contact the Florida Bar at 800-235-8619.

If you wish to report a non-accredited individual who is advising VA claimants as to how to obtain VA benefits (or to report any individual who is charging a fee to file initial VA applications), you may contact the VA Office of General Counsel at 202-461-7699.

Notes

[1] Webpage: "Our Veterans — Fast Facts." Florida Department of Veterans Affairs. Accessed December 8, 2016. http://FloridaVets.org/our-veterans/profilefast-facts/

[2] Webpage: "About VA." U.S. Department of Veterans Affairs. Accessed December 8, 2016. https://www.va.gov/landing2_about.htm

[3] Webpage: "Office of Budget – Annual Budget Submission." U.S. Department of Veterans Affairs. Accessed December 8, 2016. http://www.va.gov/budget/products.asp

[4] Webpage, PDF: Adapted from: *VA History in Brief*, Accessed December 8, 2016. U.S. Department of Veterans Affairs. https://www.va.gov/opa/publications/archives/docs/history_in_brief.pdf

[5] Webpage: "U.S. Sill Paying a Civil War Pension." Curt Mills, *U.S, News & World Report*. Accessed December 8, 2016. http://www.usnews.com/news/articles/2016-08-08/civil-war-vets-pension-still-remains-on-governments-payroll-151-years-after-last-shot-fired

[6] Webpage: Office of Research & Development. "VA Research on Prosthetics/Limb Loss." U.S. Department of Veterans Affairs. Accessed December 8, 2016. http://www.research.va.gov/topics/prosthetics.cfm

[7] Webpage: "Statistics about the Vietnam War." History.com, Vietnam Helicopter Flight Crew Network. Accessed December 8, 2016. http://www.vhfcn.org/stat.html

[8] [DOC] M21-1MR, Part I, Chapter 5, Section I; Court of Appeals for Veterans Claims (CAVC). Department of Veterans Affairs (VA). Accessed December 8, 2016.

[9] Webpage: "Military Health History Pocket Card." U.S. Department of Veterans Affairs. Accessed December 8, 2016. http://www.va.gov/oaa/pocketcard/m-gulfwar.asp

[10] Webpage: "Operation Enduring Freedom Exposures." Department of Veterans Affairs. Accessed April 12, 1017. https://www.publichealth.va.gov/exposures/wars-operations/oef.asp

[11] Webpage, PDF: *Profile of Veterans: 2014 Data from the American Community Survey.* United States Department of Veterans Affairs, prepared by the National Center for Veterans Analysis and Statistics, March 2016; Accessed December 8, 2016. http://www.va.gov/vetdata/docs/SpecialReports/Profile_of_Veterans_2014.pdf

[12] Webpage: "National Center for Veterans Analysis and Statistics, Veteran Population." U.S. Department of Veterans Affairs. Accessed December 8, 2016. http://www.va.gov/vetdata/veteran_population.asp

[13] 38 U.S.C. §101(2); 38 C.F.R. §3.1(d).

[14] Webpage, PDF: *Veterans Affairs: Presumptive Service Connection and Disability Compensation.* Congressional Research Service, 7-5700, www.crs.gov, R41405. Accessed December 8, 2016. https://www.fas.org/sgp/crs/misc/R41405.pdf

[15] Webpage, PDF: *Disability Compensation, Special Monthly Compensation.* Department of Veterans Affairs, February 2015. Accessed December 8, 2016. http://www.benefits.va.gov/BENEFITS/factsheets/serviceconnected/smc.pdf

[16] Webpage: "Compensation, Veterans Compensation Benefits Rate Tables." Effective December 1, 2016. Accessed April 12, 2017. http://www.benefits.va.gov/COMPENSATION/resources_comp01.asp

[17] John R. Frazier, *Protecting your Family's Assets: How to Legally Use Medicaid to Pay for Nursing Home and Assisted Living Care,* 2nd ed. Florida, Rainbow Books Inc., 2012, 108–111 (adapted).

[18] Webpage: "Compensation, Automobile Allowance." U.S. Department of Veterans Affairs." Accessed December 8, 2016. http://www.benefits.va.gov/compensation/claims-special-auto-allowance.asp

[19] Webpage: "Office of Public and Intergovernmental Affairs, Federal Benefits for Veterans, Dependents and Survivors, Disability Compensation; Chapter 2, 'Service-connected Disabilities.'" U.S. Department of Veterans Affairs. Accessed December 8, 2016. http://www.va.gov/opa/publications/benefits_book/benefits_chap02.asp

[20] Ibid

[21] Webpage, PDF: *VA Life Insurance Programs for Veterans and Servicemembers.* Department of Veterans Affairs, February 2016. Accessed December 8, 2016. http://www.benefits.va.gov/INSURANCE/docs/2016_VALifeBook.pdf

[22] Webpage: "Compensation, Veteran Records Destroyed by Fire in 1973." U.S. Department of Veterans Affairs. Accessed December 8, 2016. http://www.benefits.va.gov/COMPENSATION/NPRC1973Fire.asp

[23] John R. Frazier, *Protecting your Family's Assets*, 115.

[24] Webpage: "Medicaid." Florida Department of Children and Families. Accessed December 8, 2016. http://www.myflfamilies.com/service-programs/access-florida-food-medical-assistance-cash/medicaid

[25] Webpage, Genworth: "Compare Long Term Care Costs Across the United States." Accessed April 13, 2017. https://www.genworth.com/about-us/industry-expertise/cost-of-care.html

[26]   Webpage, PDF: *May–December 2015 Summary of Changes.* Florida Department of Children and Families. Accessed December 8, 2016. http://www.dcf.state.fl.us/programs/access/docs/esspolicymanual/May-December2015SummaryofChanges.pdf

[27] Webpage: "Office of General Counsel." U.S. Department of Veterans Affairs. Accessed December 8, 2016. https://www.va.gov/OGC/

[28] Webpage, PDF: *Department of Veterans Affairs Office of General Counsel.* U.S. Department of Veterans Affairs 5/23/2016. Accessed December 8, 2016. http://www.va.gov/OGC/docs/AboutOGC2015.pdf

[29] Webpage, PDF: *What Veterans and Their Families Should Know When Applying for Department of Veterans Affairs (VA) Pension Benefits.* U.S. Department of Veterans Affairs. Accessed December 8, 2016. http://benefits.va.gov/PENSION/Pensionprograminfo.pdf

[30] Webpage: "Eligible Wartime Periods." U.S. Department of Veterans Affairs. Accessed December 8, 2016. http://www.benefits.va.gov/pension/wartimeperiod.asp

[31] Webpage: "H.R. 5588 (114th): Veterans' Compensation COLA Act of 2016." GovTrack.us., 114th Congress, 2015–2017. Accessed December 6, 2016. https://www.govtrack.us/congress/bills/114/hr5588

[32] Webpage: "AO73 — Proposed Rule — Net Worth, Asset Transfers, and Income Exclusions for Needs-Based Benefits." Regulations.gov. Accessed December 7, 2016. https://www.regulations.gov/document?D=VA-2015-VBA-0003-0001

[33] Webpage: "AO73 — Proposed Rule — Net Worth, Asset Transfers, and Income Exclusions for Needs-Based Benefits." Regulations.gov. Accessed December 7, 2016 at https://www.regulations.gov/document?D=VA-2015-VBA-0003-0001

[34] Webpage: "The Debt to the Penny and Who Holds It." TreasuryDirect, United States Department of the Treasury. Accessed December 3, 2016. https://www.treasurydirect.gov/govt/reports/pd/pd_debttothepenny.htm

[35] Webpage: "National Debt." JustFacts.com. Accessed December 7, 2016. http://www.justfacts.com/nationaldebt.asp

[36] Webpage, PDF: *Summary of The Budget and Economic Outlook: 2016 to 2026.* Office of Budget, January 19, 2016. Accessed December 7, 2016.   https://www.cbo.gov/sites/default/files/114th-congress-2015-2016/reports/51129-2016_Outlook_Summary.pdf

[37] Webpage: "Office of Budget, Annual Budget Submission." Department of Veterans Affairs. Accessed December 7, 2016. http://www.va.gov/budget/products.asp

[38] Webpage: "Debt is Biggest Threat to National Security, Chairman Says." DOD News, U.S. Department of Defense. Accessed December 8, 2016. http://archive.defense.gov/news/newsarticle.aspx?id=65432

[39] Florida Supreme Court Advisory Opinion No. SC14-211, Jan. 15, 2015.

[40] Florida Statutes Title XXXII. Regulation of Professions and Occupations, § 454.23: Attorneys At Law; Penalties.

Index

About John R. Frazier, J.D., LL.M.

John R. Frazier, J.D., LL.M.

Cydonia Studios Photography

John R. Frazier graduated Cum Laude from Hampden-Sydney College in Virginia with a B.A. in Economics in 1986. He received his Master's degree in Business Administration from Virginia Tech in 1994; graduated Cum Laude from the University of Toledo, College of Law in 1997; and received his LL.M. in Taxation from the University of Florida, College of Law in 1998.

John is licensed to practice Law in both Florida and Georgia, and he practices primarily in the fields of Elder Law, Medicaid Planning, Veterans Benefits Law, Estate Planning, Asset Protection, Taxation, and Business Organizations.

John is admitted to practice before the United States Court of Appeals for Veterans Claims, and he is accredited by the Veterans Administration to assist VA claimants present, prepare and prosecute claims with the VA. He is also a member of the National Academy of Elder Law Attorneys, the Academy of Florida Elder Law Attorneys, and the Florida Bar Elder Law Section.

As the son of a physician and military officer, and with four brothers, John traveled widely in the U.S.A. and abroad while growing up. John's exposure to different cultures has created a lifelong interest in learning about other regions of the world. His current interests include the study of Latin America, Spanish music, Italian music and reading.

John R. Frazier may be reached through his website:

www.EstateLegalPlanning.com

About Joseph F. Pippen, Jr., J.D.

Joseph F. Pippen, Jr., J.D.

Joseph Franklin Pippen, Jr., Attorney, was born in 1947 in Richmond, Virginia. He graduated from Virginia Tech in 1969 with a degree in economics. He also served in the National Guard as a Captain of a combat engineering group. From 1969 until 1980, he was an executive in management positions in the fields of manufacturing, production control, marketing, purchasing, finance and public relations.

Photo by Beverly Pippen

From 1980 through part of 1982, Joe Pippen served as general manager of Micro-Plate, Inc. of Florida and helped guide the small, high-tech company into becoming a major force in the printed circuit-board industry.

Joe Pippen graduated from the University of Baltimore Law School in 1975 with a Juris Doctorate and has been practicing law since 1982. His law firm has grown to offices in Largo, St. Petersburg, Bradenton,

Sun City Center, Tampa, Zephyrhills, Lakeland, Davenport, Clermont, Leesburg, Deland, Fruitland Park and The Villages. Although Attorney Joe Pippen is an estate planning attorney, his law firm consists of nine attorneys who practice in the areas of estate and tax planning, probate, real estate, asset protection, Medicaid, bankruptcy, guardianship, and family law issues. He has also taught Business Law and Management at Anne Arundel Community College and at St. Petersburg College.

Besides his noteworthy career and business accomplishments, Pippen has numerous other achievements to his credit. He has been honored four times as one of the "Outstanding Men of America," has been listed in *Who's Who of Finance and Industry* and *Who's Who in American Law*. He also has been cited as one of the "Outstanding Volunteer Activists." Of all his achievements, Pippen is most proud of the millions of dollars he has raised for the United Way and his volunteer role with young people and the free enterprise system through the Hugh O'Brian Youth Foundation.

Pippen is a noted speaker and lecturer on motivational and personal dynamic subjects, as well as management and legal topics. He provides weekly seminars that anyone can attend at no cost. His weekly column, "Ask An Attorney," appeared in several local newspapers, and he has hosted a continuous weekly radio call-in show, titled "Ask An Attorney," since 1985. He has also hosted a national call-in radio show with the same title on the Sun Radio Network.

He is married to his high school sweetheart, Beverly, and they have two sons, Trey and Troy, and two grandsons, Austin and Trevor. They presently reside in Largo, Florida.

Law Offices of Joseph F. Pippen, Jr. & Associates
1920 East Bay Drive
Largo, FL 33771
1-800-226-3529
www.AttyPip.com